Math and Test Taking Grade 7
A Best Value Book™

Written by
Dawn Talluto Jacobi

Edited by
Kelley Wingate Levy

© Carson-Dellosa CD-3757

ISBN 0-88724-538-2

Contents

Math and Test Taking

Written by Dawn Talluto Jacobi
Edited by Kelley Wingate Levy

About the Author

Dawn Talluto Jacobi is currently working as a math teacher of the gifted at Destrehan High School in Destrehan, Louisiana. She earned a degree in Mathematics from the University of New Orleans and is currently pursuing a Master's degree in Gifted Education. Eternally grateful for the many blessings bestowed upon her, Dawn thanks her husband, Jimmy, and their beautiful children, Kara, Eric, Kaitlin, and Matthew, for their inspiration and support.

Perfect for school or home, every **Kelley Wingate Best Value Book**™ has been designed to help students master the skills necessary to succeed. Each book is packed with reproducible test pages, 96 cut-apart flash cards, and supplemental resource pages full of valuable information, ideas, and activities. These activities may be used as classroom or homework activities, or as enrichment material for a math program.

The purpose of this book is to provide conceptual, computational, and applied mathematical skills practice while reinforcing positive test taking strategies. The format and types of activities have been patterned after those in standardized tests such as Stanford Achievement, LEAP, Iowa Test of Basic Skills, and other state and nationally based achievement tests. The activities have been sequenced to facilitate successful completion of the assigned tasks, thus building the confidence and self-esteem students need to meet academic challenges.

The practice tests in this book cover the range of cognitive skills from basic concepts, to computation skills, to applied mathematical concepts. Practice tests at the end of each section provide opportunities for cumulative review. These practice tests may be administered in various ways. One method is to give students the activities consecutively, each cognitive skill building upon the previous. Alternately, select one sheet from each skill category and give students this packet, a comprehensive approach similar to many standardized tests. Once students are familiar with the practice test format, consider giving them timed practice tests, since many standardized tests are timed. Take into consideration the length and difficulty of the test, as well as the competency level of the test-takers. Cumulative practice tests are included at the end of each skill section, and at the end of the book. Extra tests may be assembled by selecting one or two pages from each of the three skill areas and administering them together.

Test Taking Strategies

Below are some suggestions for improving students' test-taking performance; you may wish to share some or all of these with your students:

- Keep a few pieces of scratch paper beside your test for working out problems.

- Use a ruler or index card to keep your place on the answer sheet.

- Have an extra sharpened pencil and a good eraser ready.

- Read the problems carefully. Decide if you know the answer before you look at the choices.

- Read all the choices, even if the first seems correct. If you don't know which answer is right, cross off the ones you know are wrong. Then, pick from the remaining choices.

- If your answer is not one of the choices, go back over your work. If you are certain your answer is correct, mark the space for NH (not here).

- Answers should be marked by completely darkening the circle that corresponds to the selected choice.

- Always put down an answer. (If you aren't sure about the answer, make a good guess! If you leave a problem blank, you know it will be wrong. A guess might just be correct!)

Using the Answer Sheet

Included at the end of this book, preceding the flash cards, is a universal answer sheet designed specifically for use with this book. Each sheet has enough answer columns for multiple test pages. When administering a test, reproduce this page for your students, making sure to specify at the top of each answer column the page number corresponding to the particular test they are taking. Optionally, these answer sheets can be reused until every column is filled. Space is also provided for test-scoring feedback.

Flash Card Ideas and Activities

Included in the back of this book are 96 flash cards ideal for individual review, group solving sessions, or as part of timed, sequential, or grouped tests. Pull out the flash cards and cut them apart or, if you have access to a paper cutter, use that to cut them into individual cards. Here are just a few of the ways you may want to use these flash cards:

- Play "Around the World with Flash Cards," the object of which is to be the first student to circle the room and return to his own seat. Have two students stand at their desks. Show them one flash card. The first to correctly answer the flash card problem advances and stands beside the next seat in line. The student in that seat stands. Show these two students a flash card, and repeat the process. The winner continues to advance and challenge, in which case he sits down and the new winner advances to face a new flash card and the next student.

- Hold a "Math Challenge." Divide the class into two teams and have a representative from each team stand at the front of the room beside a desk and attempt to be the first to answer a flash card problem. The student who is able to answer the question first can tap the desk (or ring a bell) to signal readiness to give an answer. Award points for correct answers. If the student answers incorrectly, allow the other team a chance to answer.

- Use a timer or stopwatch to record how many problems a student can answer correctly in a certain amount of time. Review incorrect answers and repeat the exercise. Provide rewards for improved scores.

- Give students a card with a math fact on it. Have them write out the other members of that fact family, or brainstorm other math problems that have the same answer.

- Use flash cards as impromptu quizzes. Give each student three to five cards attached to an answer sheet that he can complete and return. Vary the selection of cards given to each student for each quiz.

- Post a certain number of cards, daily or weekly, as bonus questions or for extra credit.

Name _____

Directions

Read each question and choose the correct answer. Mark the space for the answer you have chosen. Mark NH if the answer is not here.

---

1. What is the numeral for ten thousand, ten?

    a. 1,010
    b. 10,010
    c. 100,010
    d. 1,000,010
    e. NH

6. What is the numeral for ninety-four thousand, thirteen?

    f. 94,013
    g. 9,413
    h. 904,012
    j. 940,013
    k. NH

---

2. What is the numeral for eighty thousand, forty-six?

    f. 846
    g. 8,046
    h. 8,406
    j. 80,046
    k. NH

7. What is the numeral for sixty thousand, thirty?

    a. 600,030
    b. 60,030
    c. 6,030
    d. 6,300
    e. NH

---

3. What is the numeral for nine thousand, twelve?

    a. 912,000
    b. 9,120
    c. 90,012
    d. 9,012
    e. NH

8. What is the numeral for nine hundred thousand, two hundred?

    f. 9,000,200
    g. 900,200
    h. 90,200
    j. 9,002
    k. NH

---

4. What is the numeral for fifty thousand, thirty?

    f. 5,030
    g. 53,000
    h. 500,030
    j. 50,030
    k. NH

9. What is the numeral for five hundred seventy thousand, fifty?

    a. 507,050
    b. 50,750
    c. 57,050
    d. 570,050
    e. NH

---

5. What is the numeral for seventy-two thousand, one?

    a. 7,201
    b. 70,201
    c. 72,001
    d. 720,001
    e. NH

10. What is the numeral for fifty million, seven hundred thousand, eleven?

    f. 50,711,000
    g. 50,070,011
    h. 50,700,011
    j. 5,700,011
    k. NH

Directions
Read each question and choose the correct answer. Mark the space for the answer you have chosen. Mark NH if the answer is not here.

---

1. What is another way of writing 2^3?

   a. **6**
   b. **2 + 2 + 2**
   c. **2 x 2 x 2**
   d. **2 x 3**
   e. **NH**

6. What is another way of writing $\frac{2}{3}$?

   f. $\frac{5}{9}$ g. $\frac{4}{9}$ h. $\frac{5}{6}$ j. $\frac{4}{6}$ **k. NH**

---

2. What is another way of writing 4^3?

   f. **12**
   g. **4 x 3**
   h. **3 x 3 x 3 x 3**
   j. **4 x 4 x 4**
   k. **NH**

7. What is another way of writing 5 + (2 + 1)?

   a. **(5 + 2) + 3**
   b. **(5 + 2) + 1**
   c. **(5 + 2) + (5 + 1)**
   d. **(5 + 1) + 3**
   e. **NH**

---

3. What is another way of writing 0.3?

   a. $\frac{3}{1}$ b. $\frac{3}{10}$ c. $\frac{3}{100}$ d. $\frac{3}{3}$ **e. NH**

8. What is another way of writing (4 + 6) + 5?

   f. **10 + (6 + 5)**
   g. **4 + (6 + 11)**
   h. **(4 + 6) + 11**
   j. **4 + (6 + 5)**
   k. **NH**

---

4. What is another way of writing $\frac{14}{3}$?

   f. $1\frac{4}{3}$ g. $3\frac{2}{3}$ h. $4\frac{2}{3}$ j. $4\frac{1}{3}$ **k. NH**

9. What is another way of writing 5 x (2 + 7)?

   a. **(5 x 2) + 7**
   b. **(5 x 2) + (5 x 7)**
   c. **(5 x 7) + 2**
   d. **(5 x 2) + (5 x 9)**
   e. **NH**

---

5. What is another way of writing 0.07?

   a. $\frac{7}{100}$ b. $\frac{7}{10}$ c. $\frac{7}{1}$ d. $\frac{7}{7}$ **e. NH**

10. What is another way of writing 9 x (6 + 1)?

   f. **(9 x 6) + (9 x 1)**
   g. **(9 x 6) + 1**
   h. **(9 + 6) x (9 + 1)**
   j. **(9 x 1) + 6**
   k. **NH**

Directions
Read each question and choose the correct answer. Mark the space for the answer you have chosen. Mark NH if the answer is not here.

1. What is another way of writing 6?

   a. $8 - (5 \times 3)$
   b. $3 + (12 \div 4)$
   c. $25 \div 5 \times 2$
   d. $12 \div 6 \times 4$
   e.   NH

2. What is another way of writing 12?

   f. $6 + (12 \div 6)$
   g. $(15 \div 3) + 9$
   h. $4 + 2 \times 2$
   j. $(6 \div 2) \times 4$
   k.   NH

3. What is another way of writing 2?

   a. $9 - (14 \div 7)$
   b. $24 \div 8 + 1$
   c. $5 - (6 \div 3)$
   d. $8 \div 2 \div 2$
   e.   NH

4. What is another way of writing 7?

   f. $3 + (2 \times 2)$
   g. $10 + 4 \div 2$
   h. $27 \div 3 - 1$
   j. $5 + (8 \div 2)$
   k.   NH

5. What is another way of writing 5?

   a. $2 + (6 \div 2)$
   b. $20 \div 5 + 2$
   c. $(7 \times 2) - 8$
   d. $10 - (2 \times 3)$
   e.   NH

6. What is another way of writing 3^4?

   f. 3×4
   g. $4 \times 4 \times 4$
   h. $3 \times 3 \times 3 \times 3$
   j. $3 + 3 + 3 + 3$
   k.   NH

7. What is another way of writing 5^3?

   a. $5 \times 5 \times 5$
   b. 5×3
   c. $3 \times 3 \times 3 \times 3 \times 3$
   d. 15×3
   e.   NH

8. What fraction is another way of writing $\frac{1}{4}$?

   f. $\frac{1}{2}$ g. $\frac{5}{24}$ h. $\frac{3}{16}$ j. $\frac{8}{32}$ k. NH

9. What fraction is another way of writing $\frac{7}{8}$?

   a. $\frac{49}{64}$ b. $\frac{17}{18}$ c. $\frac{35}{40}$ d. $\frac{14}{24}$ e. NH

10. What fraction is another way of writing $\frac{2}{3}$?

   f. $\frac{3}{5}$ g. $\frac{4}{9}$ h. $\frac{10}{12}$ j. $\frac{4}{6}$ k. NH

Directions

Read each question and choose the correct answer. Mark the space for the answer you have chosen. Mark NH if the answer is not here.

---

1. What fraction is another name for $8\frac{1}{2}$?

a. $\frac{2}{1}$ b. $\frac{7}{16}$ c. $\frac{81}{2}$ d. $\frac{17}{2}$ e. NH

6. What fraction is another name for 3%?

f. $\frac{3}{1,000}$ g. $\frac{3}{100}$ h. $\frac{3}{12}$ j. $\frac{3}{1}$ k. NH

---

2. What fraction is another name for 7.15?

f. $7\frac{15}{1,000}$ g. $7\frac{7}{15}$ h. $7\frac{3}{20}$ j. $7\frac{5}{10}$ k. NH

7. What decimal is another name for $\frac{17}{100}$?

a. 17.0
b. 1.70
c. 1.7
d. 0.17
e. NH

---

3. What fraction is another name for 0.14?

a. $1\frac{2}{5}$ b. $\frac{1}{14}$ c. $\frac{7}{50}$ d. $\frac{14}{1,000}$ e. NH

8. What decimal is another name for $\frac{1}{4}$?

f. 1.4
g. 0.14
h. 2.5
j. 0.25
k. NH

---

4. What fraction is another name for 0.009?

f. $\frac{9}{1,000}$ g. $\frac{9}{10,000}$ h. $\frac{9}{100}$ j. $\frac{9}{10}$ k. NH

9. What percent is another name for 0.6?

a. 0.6%
b. 6%
c. 60%
d. 600%
e. NH

---

5. What fraction is another name for 19%?

a. $\frac{19}{100}$ b. $\frac{19}{1,000}$ c. $1\frac{9}{10}$ d. $\frac{19}{10}$ e. NH

10. What percent is another name for 1.25?

f. 1.25%
g. 12.5%
h. 125%
j. 1,250%
k. NH

Name _____   Skill: Place Value

Directions
Read each question and choose the correct answer. Mark the space for the answer you have chosen. Mark NH if the answer is not here.

---

1. What does the 3 in 53,471 represent?

   a. 3
   b. 300
   c. 3,000
   d. 30,000
   e. NH

6. What is the simplest name for
$$(5 \times 10^2) + (2 \times 10) + (0 \times 1)?$$

   f. 5,002
   g. 521
   h. 520
   j. 5,020
   k. NH

---

2. What does the 8 in 682,106 represent?

   f. 800,000
   g. 80,000
   h. 8,000
   j. 80
   k. NH

7. What is the simplest name for
$$(4 \times 10^3) + (7 \times 10^2) + (0 \times 10) + (3 \times 1)?$$

   a. 40,703
   b. 4,703
   c. 4,730
   d. 400,703
   e. NH

---

3. What does the 4 in 1,705,429 represent?

   a. 40,000
   b. 400
   c. 40
   d. 4,000
   e. NH

8. What is the simplest name for
$$(6 \times 10^3) + (0 \times 10^2) + (8 \times 10) + (2 \times 1)?$$

   f. 6,082
   g. 60,082
   h. 6,820
   j. 60,802
   k. NH

---

4. What does the 1 in 4,162,309 represent?

   f. 1,000,000
   g. 100
   h. 10,000
   j. 100,000
   k. NH

9. What is the simplest name for
$$(9 \times 10^3) + (0 \times 10^2) + (0 \times 10) + (4 \times 1)?$$

   a. 9,004
   b. 90,004
   c. 90,040
   d. 90,400
   e. NH

---

5. What does the 3 in 143,657,890 represent?

   a. 3
   b. 300,000
   c. 3,000,000
   d. 30,000,000
   e. NH

10. What is the simplest name for: $(3 \times 10^4) +$ $(2 \times 10^3) + (0 \times 10^2) + (2 \times 10) + (0 \times 1)?$

   f. 300,220
   g. 302,020
   h. 3,220
   j. 32,020
   k. NH

Directions
Read each question and choose the correct answer. Mark the space for the answer you have chosen. Mark NH if the answer is not here.

---

1. What does the 5 in 1.85 represent?

  a. 5 ones
  b. 5 hundredths
  c. 5 tenths
  d. 5 thousandths
  e. NH

6. What number is 2 tenths more than 45.36?

  f. 47.36
  g. 45.56
  h. 45.38
  j. 55.36
  k. NH

---

2. What does the 1 in 206.1 represent?

  f. 1 one
  g. 1 hundred
  h. 1 hundredth
  j. 1 tenth
  k. NH

7. What number is 5 tenths more than 5,814.341?

  a. 5,864.341
  b. 5,814.391
  c. 5,819.341
  d. 5,814.841
  e. NH

---

3. What does the 2 in 35.502 represent?

  a. 2 ten thousandths
  b. 2 thousandths
  c. 2 hundredths
  d. 2 tenths
  e. NH

8. What number is 3 tenths more than 66.524?

  f. 66.824
  g. 66.554
  h. 96.524
  j. 69.524
  k. NH

---

4. What does the 4 in 1,628.8425 represent?

  f. 4 tenths
  g. 4 thousandths
  h. 4 hundredths
  j. 4 ten thousandths
  k. NH

9. What number is 2 hundredths more than 397.304?

  a. 597.304
  b. 397.504
  c. 397.324
  d. 397.524
  e. NH

---

5. What does the 7 in 52,384.0957 represent?

  a. 7 hundredths
  b. 7 ten thousandths
  c. 7 thousandths
  d. 7 hundred thousandths
  e. NH

10. What number is 4 hundredths more than 8,326.41?

  f. 8,326.81
  g. 8,326.85
  h. 8,326.45
  j. 8,726.41
  k. NH

Name _____

Directions

Read each question and choose the correct answer. Mark the space for the answer you have chosen. Mark NH if the answer is not here.

---

1. What is 136.83 rounded to the nearest whole number?

    a. 136.8
    b. 137
    c. 136
    d. 140
    e. NH

6. What is 93,840 rounded to the nearest thousand?

    f. 94,000
    g. 93,000
    h. 93,800
    j. 90,000
    k. NH

---

2. What is 3,304.49 rounded to the nearest whole number?

    f. 3,304
    g. 3,305.49
    h. 3,304.5
    j. 3,305
    k. NH

7. What is 843,499 rounded to the nearest ten thousand?

    a. 843,000
    b. 840,000
    c. 800,000
    d. 850,000
    e. NH

---

3. What is 80.51 rounded to the nearest whole number?

    a. 81
    b. 80.5
    c. 80
    d. 80.51
    e. NH

8. What is 207,615 rounded to the nearest ten thousand?

    f. 208,000
    g. 210,000
    h. 200,000
    j. 207,600
    k. NH

---

4. What is 3462.8 rounded to the nearest ten?

    f. 3,462
    g. 3,463
    h. 3,460
    j. 3,500
    k. NH

9. What is 3,582,641.6 rounded to the nearest thousand?

    a. 3,583,000
    b. 3,582,600
    c. 3,580,000
    d. 3,600,000
    e. NH

---

5. What is 52,894 rounded to the nearest hundred?

    a. 52,900
    b. 52,890
    c. 52,800
    d. 53,000
    e. NH

10. What is 92,852.36 rounded to the nearest hundred?

    f. 92,800
    g. 92,900
    h. 92,850
    j. 93,000
    k. NH

Name _____

Directions

Read each question and choose the correct answer. Mark the space for the answer you have chosen. Mark NH if the answer is not here.

---

1. Which is the least common denominator for $\frac{1}{2}$, $\frac{2}{3}$, and $\frac{3}{4}$?

   a. 6
   b. 8
   c. 12
   d. 24
   e. NH

6. Which is the least common denominator for $\frac{1}{4}$, $\frac{5}{6}$, and $\frac{5}{8}$?

   f. 12
   g. 24
   h. 48
   j. 72
   k. NH

---

2. Which is the least common denominator for $\frac{1}{3}$, $\frac{5}{6}$, and $\frac{4}{9}$?

   f. 6
   g. 9
   h. 18
   j. 54
   k. NH

7. Which is the least common denominator for $\frac{2}{3}$, $\frac{8}{9}$, and $\frac{1}{12}$?

   a. 9
   b. 18
   c. 27
   d. 36
   e. NH

---

3. Which is the least common denominator for $\frac{1}{2}$, $\frac{3}{4}$, and $\frac{3}{5}$?

   a. 10
   b. 20
   c. 40
   d. 100
   e. NH

8. Which is the least common denominator for $\frac{3}{4}$, $\frac{2}{5}$, and $\frac{5}{6}$?

   f. 20
   g. 40
   h. 60
   j. 120
   k. NH

---

4. Which is the least common denominator for $\frac{2}{3}$, $\frac{4}{5}$, and $\frac{3}{10}$?

   f. 10
   g. 15
   h. 30
   j. 60
   k. NH

9. Which is the least common denominator for $\frac{2}{3}$, $\frac{1}{6}$, and $\frac{7}{10}$?

   a. 18
   b. 30
   c. 60
   d. 180
   e. NH

---

5. Which is the least common denominator for $\frac{3}{4}$, $\frac{5}{8}$, and $\frac{7}{12}$?

   a. 12
   b. 16
   c. 24
   d. 48
   e. NH

10. Which is the least common denominator for $\frac{1}{2}$, $\frac{5}{6}$, and $\frac{9}{10}$?

   f. 10
   g. 30
   h. 60
   j. 120
   k. NH

Name _____

Directions

Read each question and choose the correct answer. Mark the space for the answer you have chosen. Mark NH if the answer is not here.

---

1. Which fraction is greatest?

     a. $\frac{1}{3}$ b. $\frac{1}{2}$ c. $\frac{1}{4}$ d. $\frac{1}{5}$ e. NH

---

6. Which group of fractions is in order from least to greatest?

   f. $\frac{1}{4}, \frac{1}{3}, \frac{1}{2}$ g. $\frac{1}{3}, \frac{1}{4}, \frac{1}{2}$

   h. $\frac{1}{2}, \frac{1}{3}, \frac{1}{4}$ j. $\frac{1}{2}, \frac{1}{4}, \frac{1}{3}$

             k. NH

---

2. Which fraction is greatest?

     f. $\frac{1}{2}$ g. $\frac{5}{6}$ h. $\frac{3}{4}$ j. $\frac{3}{5}$ k. NH

---

7. Which group of fractions is in order from least to greatest?

   a. $\frac{4}{7}, \frac{1}{2}, \frac{2}{5}$ b. $\frac{4}{7}, \frac{2}{5}, \frac{1}{2}$

   c. $\frac{1}{2}, \frac{2}{5}, \frac{4}{7}$ d. $\frac{2}{5}, \frac{1}{2}, \frac{4}{7}$

             e. NH

---

3. Which fraction is greatest?

     a. $\frac{2}{3}$ b. $\frac{3}{4}$ c. $\frac{7}{9}$ d. $\frac{5}{8}$ e. NH

---

8. Which group of fractions is in order from least to greatest?

   f. $\frac{3}{4}, \frac{6}{10}, \frac{7}{8}$ g. $\frac{6}{10}, \frac{3}{4}, \frac{7}{8}$

   h. $\frac{3}{4}, \frac{7}{8}, \frac{6}{10}$ j. $\frac{7}{8}, \frac{6}{10}, \frac{3}{4}$

             k. NH

---

4. Which fraction is greatest?

     f. $\frac{7}{10}$ g. $\frac{5}{6}$ h. $\frac{3}{4}$ j. $\frac{7}{8}$ k. NH

---

9. Which group of fractions is in order from least to greatest?

   a. $\frac{3}{7}, \frac{6}{11}, \frac{8}{16}$ b. $\frac{3}{7}, \frac{8}{16}, \frac{6}{11}$

   c. $\frac{6}{11}, \frac{3}{7}, \frac{8}{16}$ d. $\frac{8}{16}, \frac{3}{7}, \frac{6}{11}$

             e. NH

---

5. Which fraction is greatest?

     a. $\frac{5}{9}$ b. $\frac{6}{7}$ c. $\frac{4}{7}$ d. $\frac{5}{12}$ e. NH

---

10. Which group of fractions is in order from least to greatest?

   f. $\frac{1}{10}, \frac{1}{12}, \frac{1}{14}$ g. $\frac{1}{12}, \frac{1}{10}, \frac{1}{14}$

   h. $\frac{1}{14}, \frac{1}{12}, \frac{1}{10}$ j. $\frac{1}{10}, \frac{1}{14}, \frac{1}{12}$

             k. NH

Name _____

Directions
Read each question and choose the correct answer. Mark the space for the answer you have chosen. Mark NH if the answer is not here.

---

1. What fraction is in its simplest form?

a. $\frac{3}{12}$ b. $\frac{3}{7}$ c. $\frac{6}{9}$ d. $\frac{6}{8}$ e. NH

6. What is the simplest form of $\frac{12}{9}$?

f. $1\frac{3}{9}$ g. $1\frac{2}{9}$ h. $1\frac{2}{3}$ j. $1\frac{1}{3}$ k. NH

---

2. What fraction is in its simplest form?

f. $\frac{5}{9}$ g. $\frac{12}{18}$ h. $\frac{9}{12}$ j. $\frac{6}{15}$ k. NH

7. What is the simplest form of $\frac{14}{3}$?

a. $4\frac{2}{3}$ b. $4\frac{1}{3}$ c. $3\frac{1}{3}$ d. $3\frac{2}{3}$ e. NH

---

3. What fraction is in its simplest form?

a. $\frac{3}{15}$ b. $\frac{6}{18}$ c. $\frac{4}{12}$ d. $\frac{8}{9}$ e. NH

8. What is the simplest form of $\frac{34}{6}$?

f. $5\frac{4}{6}$ g. $5\frac{2}{3}$ h. $6\frac{2}{6}$ j. $6\frac{1}{3}$ k. NH

---

4. What fraction is in its simplest form?

f. $\frac{9}{27}$ g. $\frac{6}{15}$ h. $\frac{4}{9}$ j. $\frac{12}{15}$ k. NH

9. What is the simplest form of $\frac{64}{12}$?

a. $\frac{16}{3}$ b. $5\frac{1}{3}$ c. $6\frac{1}{12}$ d. $5\frac{4}{12}$ e. NH

---

5. What fraction is in its simplest form?

a. $\frac{8}{12}$ b. $\frac{3}{18}$ c. $\frac{4}{11}$ d. $\frac{6}{21}$ e. NH

10. What is the simplest form of $\frac{22}{4}$?

f. $2\frac{2}{4}$ g. $5\frac{2}{4}$ h. $5\frac{1}{2}$ j. $4\frac{1}{2}$ k. NH

Directions

Read each question and choose the correct answer. Mark the space for the answer you have chosen. Mark NH if the answer is not here.

1. Which is a prime number?

    a. 4
    b. 9
    c. 13
    d. 12
    e. NH

2. Which is <u>not</u> a prime number?

    f. 5
    g. 33
    h. 41
    j. 17
    k. NH

3. Which is a pair of prime numbers?

    a. (5, 11)
    b. (7, 8)
    c. (6, 13)
    d. (9, 29)
    e. NH

4. Which is a pair of prime numbers?

    f. (3, 17)
    g. (2, 9)
    h. (3, 15)
    j. (5, 20)
    k. NH

5. Which is a pair of prime numbers?

    a. (6, 7)
    b. (8, 11)
    c. (15, 16)
    d. (11, 29)
    e. NH

6. Which is a pair of prime numbers?

    f. (6, 10)
    g. (3, 16)
    h. (7, 19)
    j. (2, 22)
    k. NH

7. Which is a pair of prime numbers?

    a. (3, 12)
    b. (19, 23)
    c. (6, 13)
    d. (9, 17)
    e. NH

8. Which is a pair of prime numbers?

    f. (4, 17)
    g. (47, 53)
    h. (5, 48)
    j. (6, 37)
    k. NH

9. Which is a pair of prime numbers?

    a. (7, 15)
    b. (2, 6)
    c. (3, 37)
    d. (4, 19)
    e. NH

10. Which is a pair of prime numbers?

    f. (2, 21)
    g. (5, 9)
    h. (8, 11)
    j. (5, 7)
    k. NH

Name _____

Directions

Read each question and choose the correct answer. Mark the space for the answer you have chosen. Mark NH if the answer is not here.

1. What is the prime factorization of 30?

   a. 6 x 5
   b. 3 x 10
   c. 2 x 3 x 5
   d. 2 x 2 x 3 x 5
   e. NH

2. What is the prime factorization of 40?

   f. 4 x 10
   g. 2 x 2 x 2 x 2 x 10
   h. 5 x 8
   j. 2 x 2 x 2 x 5
   k. NH

3. What is the prime factorization of 64?

   a. 2 x 2 x 2 x 2 x 2 x 2
   b. 4 x 4 x 4
   c. 8 x 8
   d. 16 x 4
   e. NH

4. What is the prime factorization of 45?

   f. 3 x 3 x 5
   g. 9 x 5
   h. 2 x 3 x 9
   j. 3 x 15
   k. NH

5. What is the prime factorization of 70?

   a. 7 x 10
   b. 2 x 5 x 7
   c. 2 x 5 x 10
   d. 2 x 35
   e. NH

6. What is the prime factorization of 20?

   f. 4 x 5
   g. 2 x 3 x 5
   h. 2 x 2 x 5
   j. 2 x 10
   k. NH

7. What is the prime factorization of 28?

   a. 7 x 4
   b. 2 x 2 x 7
   c. 2 x 14
   d. 3 x 3 x 3
   e. NH

8. What is the prime factorization of 75?

   f. 5 x 15
   g. 3 x 25
   h. 3 x 5 x 5
   j. 3 x 3 x 5
   k. NH

9. What is the prime factorization of 42?

   a. 2 x 21
   b. 2 x 2 x 2 x 3
   c. 2 x 2 x 3 x 3
   d. 2 x 3 x 7
   e. NH

10. What is the prime factorization of 16?

   f. 2 x 2 x 2 x 2
   g. 4 x 4
   h. 2 x 8
   j. 2 x 2 x 2 x 3
   k. NH

Directions

Read each question and choose the correct answer. Mark the space for the answer you have chosen. Mark NH if the answer is not here.

---

1. What number is between − 3 and 1?

   a.   − 5
   b.   2
   c.   0
   d.   − 4
   e.   NH

2. What number is between − 6 and − 1?

   f.   − 8
   g.   − 2
   h.   0
   j.   5
   k.   NH

3. What number is between − 5 and − 2?

   a.   − 6
   b.   − 4
   c.   − 1
   d.   0
   e.   NH

4. What number is between −7 and − 3?

   f.   − 5
   g.   − 8
   h.   − 2
   j.   4
   k.   NH

5. What is the smallest number?

   a.   1
   b.   − 2
   c.   − 3
   d.   0
   e.   NH

6. What is the smallest number?

   f.   − 2
   g.   0
   h.   3
   j.   − 5
   k.   NH

7. What is the greatest number?

   a.   − 6
   b.   − 8
   c.   − 7
   d.   − 1
   e.   NH

8. What is the greatest number?

   f.   − 2
   g.   − 4
   h.   − 6
   j.   − 8
   k.   NH

9. What numbers are in order from least to greatest?

   a.   1, − 2, − 4
   b.   − 4, − 2,   1
   c.   − 2, − 4,   1
   d.   1, − 4, − 2
   e.   NH

10. What numbers are in order from least to greatest?

   f.   − 12, − 13, − 14
   g.   5, − 6,   7
   h.   − 14, − 13, − 12
   j.   − 3, − 1, − 2
   k.   NH

Skill: Negative Numbers

Directions
Read each question and choose the correct answer. Mark the space for the answer you have chosen. Mark NH if the answer is not here.

---

1. $4 + (-3) =$

   a. -7
   b. 7
   c. -1
   d. 1
   e.   NH

6. $(-5) \times (-5) =$

   f. -25
   g. -10
   h. 10
   j. 25
   k.   NH

---

2. $(-2) + (-3) =$

   f. -5
   g. 5
   h. -6
   j. -1
   k.   NH

7. $(-4) \times 2 =$

   a. -2
   b. -8
   c. -6
   d. 2
   e.   NH

---

3. $5 + (-8) =$

   a. 3
   b. -3
   c. -13
   d. 40
   e.   NH

8. $7 \times (-3) =$

   f. 4
   g. -21
   h. -10
   j. -4
   k.   NH

---

4. $-4 + (-4) =$

   f. -8
   g. 0
   h. 8
   j. -16
   k.   NH

9. $(-6) \times (-5) =$

   a. -30
   b. 30
   c. -11
   d. -1
   e.   NH

---

5. $(-6) + 1 =$

   a. 5
   b. -6
   c. -5
   d. 6
   e.   NH

10. $(-3) \times 12 =$

   f. 9
   g. 36
   h. -36
   j. -9
   k.   NH

Directions
Read each question and choose the correct answer. Mark the space for the answer you have chosen. Mark NH if the answer is not here.

1. Solve for "n."

$\frac{1}{4}$ x n = 1

a. $\frac{1}{4}$　　b. 4　　c. $\frac{3}{4}$　　d. $\frac{4}{4}$　　e. NH

6. Solve for "n."

n x $\frac{1}{3}$ = 1

f. 3　　g. $\frac{1}{3}$　　h. $\frac{3}{3}$　　j. $\frac{2}{3}$　　k. NH

2. Solve for "n."

$\frac{2}{3}$ x n = 0

f. 32　　g. 0　　h. 1　　j. $\frac{1}{3}$　　k. NH

7. Solve for "n."

$\frac{3}{5}$ x n = 1

a. $\frac{2}{5}$　　b. $\frac{3}{3}$　　c. $\frac{5}{3}$　　d. $\frac{5}{5}$　　e. NH

3. Solve for "n."

7 x n = 1

a. $\frac{1}{7}$　　b. $\frac{7}{1}$　　c. 6　　d. $\frac{3}{7}$　　e. NH

8. Solve for "n."

$\frac{3}{4}$ x n = 0

f. $\frac{1}{4}$　　g. 0　　h. $\frac{4}{3}$　　j. $\frac{3}{3}$　　k. NH

4. Solve for "n."

$\frac{1}{6}$ x n = 1

f. $\frac{5}{6}$　　g. $\frac{1}{6}$　　h. $\frac{6}{6}$　　j. 6　　k. NH

9. Solve for "n."

5 x (n + 2) = (5 x 3) + (5 x 2)

a. 5
b. 2
c. 3
d. 25
e. NH

5. Solve for "n."

n x 2 = 1

a. 1　　b. $\frac{2}{2}$　　c. $\frac{3}{2}$　　d. $\frac{1}{2}$　　e. NH

10. Solve for "n."

3 x (4 + n) = (3 x 4) + (3 x 7)

f. 35
g. 4
h. 10
j. 7
k. NH

Name _____

Directions

Read each question and choose the correct answer. Mark the space for the answer you have chosen. Mark NH if the answer is not here.

---

1. $2^3 =$

   a. 6
   b. 8
   c. 4
   d. 23
   e. NH

6. $5^2 + 1 =$

   f. 25
   g. 11
   h. 53
   j. 26
   k. NH

---

2. $3^4 =$

   f. 81
   g. 27
   h. 36
   j. 12
   k. NH

7. $3^3 - 2 =$

   a. 7
   b. 27
   c. 25
   d. 9
   e. NH

---

3. $7^2 =$

   a. 14
   b. 72
   c. 49
   d. 21
   e. NH

8. $2^4 - 1 =$

   f. 23
   g. 16
   h. 7
   j. 15
   k. NH

---

4. $2^5 =$

   f. 32
   g. 80
   h. 10
   j. 24
   k. NH

9. $8^2 + 3 =$

   a. 19
   b. 67
   c. 85
   d. 16
   e. NH

---

5. $6^2 =$

   a. 12
   b. 36
   c. 62
   d. 18
   e. NH

10. $2^2 - 3 =$

   f. 1
   g. 4
   h. 7
   j. 19
   k. NH

Name _____

Directions

Read each question and choose the correct answer. Mark the space for the answer you have chosen. Mark NH if the answer is not here.

---

1. What does the 6 in 5.064 represent?

   a. $\frac{6}{1}$ **b.** $\frac{6}{10}$ **c.** $\frac{6}{100}$ **d.** $\frac{6}{1000}$ **e. NH**

6. What is the least common denominator for $\frac{1}{2}$, $\frac{1}{3}$, and $\frac{5}{6}$?

  f.   2
  g.   14
  h.   12
  j.   6
  k.   **NH**

---

2. What is the simplest form of $\frac{18}{4}$?

  f. 3   **g.** $4\frac{1}{2}$ **h.** $4\frac{1}{4}$ **j.** $4\frac{2}{4}$ **k. NH**

7. Which of the following is a prime number?

  a.   2
  b.   14
  c.   21
  d.   39
  e.   **NH**

---

3. What is the numeral for sixty thousand, ten?

  a.   60,010
  b.   600,010
  c.   6,010
  d.   610,010
  e.   **NH**

8. Which group of fractions is in order from least to greatest?

  f. $\frac{4}{5}$, $\frac{8}{15}$, $\frac{7}{14}$ **g.** $\frac{7}{14}$, $\frac{8}{15}$, $\frac{4}{5}$

  h. $\frac{7}{14}$, $\frac{4}{5}$, $\frac{8}{15}$ **j.** $\frac{4}{5}$, $\frac{7}{14}$, $\frac{8}{15}$

                          k. NH

---

4. What is 406.38 rounded to the nearest tenth?

  f.   410
  g.   406.3
  h.   416
  j.   406.4
  k.   **NH**

9. $2^4 =$

  a.   16
  b.   8
  c.   24
  d.   32
  e.   **NH**

---

5. Solve for "n."

   $5 \times (n + 2) = (5 \times 4) + (5 \times 2)$

  a.   4
  b.   10
  c.   2
  d.   5
  e.   **NH**

10. Which is another way of writing $3 + (2 + 4)$?

  f.   (3 + 2) + (3 + 4)
  g.   3 + (2 + 6)
  h.   (3 + 2) + 4
  j.   (3 x 2) + (3 x 4)
  k.   **NH**

Directions

Read each question and choose the correct answer. Mark the space for the answer you have chosen. Mark NH if the answer is not here.

---

1. Which fraction is another name for $\frac{2}{5}$?

a. $\frac{4}{25}$ b. $\frac{6}{20}$ c. $2\frac{1}{2}$ d. $\frac{6}{15}$ e. NH

6. What is the prime factorization of 18?

f.   2 x 9
g.   3 x 6
h.   1 x 18
j.   2 x 3 x 3
k.   NH

---

2. What is another way of writing 5 x (3 + 9)?

f.   (5 x 3) + (5 x 9)
g.   (5 x 3) x (5 x 9)
h.   (5 x 3) + 9
j.   5 + (3 x 9)
k.   NH

7. (– 6) x (– 8) =

a.   – 48
b.   48
c.   – 14
d.   14
e.   NH

---

3. What decimal is another name for $\frac{1}{5}$?

a.   1.5
b.   0.2
c.   1.05
d.   0.15
e.   NH

8. What is another way of writing 3^3?

f.   9
g.   3 x 3 x 3
h.   3 x 3
j.   3 + 3 + 3
k.   NH

---

4. Which fraction is in its simplest form?

f. $\frac{6}{15}$ g. $\frac{10}{14}$ h. $\frac{5}{9}$ j. $\frac{7}{14}$ k. NH

9. What number is 4 tenths more than 821.35?

a.   821.75
b.   821.39
c.   851.35
d.   825.35
e.   NH

---

5. What is 834.62 rounded to the nearest whole number?

a.   835
b.   834
c.   834.6
d.   830
e.   NH

10. Solve for "n."

$\frac{6}{15}$ x n = 0

f. $\frac{3}{2}$ g. $\frac{3}{3}$ h. $\frac{1}{2}$ j. 0   k. NH

Directions

Read each question and choose the correct answer. Mark the space for the answer you have chosen. Mark NH if the answer is not here.

---

1. What decimal is another name for 17%?

    a. 17.0
    b. 1.7
    c. 1.07
    d. 0.17
    e. NH

6. Which numbers are in order from least to greatest?

    f. $-1, -4, -5$
    g. $-5, -1, -4$
    h. $-4, -1, -4$
    j. $-5, -4, -1$
    k. NH

---

2. What does the 6 in 475,612 mean?

    f. 600
    g. 6,000
    h. 60
    j. 6
    k. NH

7. $2^3 + 4 =$

    a. 12
    b. 10
    c. 16
    d. 27
    e. NH

---

3. $4 + (-6) =$

    a. 10
    b. -2
    c. -24
    d. 2
    e. NH

8. Which is another way of writing 10?

    f. 5^2
    g. $8 + (12 \div 2)$
    h. $2 + (2 \times 4)$
    j. $2 \times 2 \times 2 \times 2 \times 2$
    k. NH

---

4. What fraction is another name for 0.07?

    f. $\frac{7}{10}$ g. $\frac{7}{100}$ h. $\frac{7}{1,000}$ j. $\frac{7}{10,000}$ k. NH

9. Which is a pair of prime numbers?

    a. (7, 31)
    b. (2, 15)
    c. (5, 38)
    d. (19, 4)
    e. NH

---

5. What is the numeral for eighteen thousand, six?

    a. 180,006
    b. 18,006
    c. 1,806
    d. 1,086
    e. NH

10. What is 80,475.6737 rounded to the nearest hundred?

    f. 80,500
    g. 80,400
    h. 80,475
    j. 80,475.67
    k. NH

Directions

Read each question and choose the correct answer. Mark the space for the answer you have chosen. Mark NH if the answer is not here.

---

1. What is the simplest way to write
$(7 \times 10^3) + (0 \times 10^2) + (4 \times 10) + (0 \times 1)$?

  a. 7,040
  b. 70,040
  c. 7,004
  d. 700,400
  e. NH

6. $(-7) \times 8 =$

  f.   1
  g.   −1
  h.   56
  j.   −56
  k.   NH

---

2. What is the simplest form of $\frac{15}{9}$?

  f. $1\frac{6}{9}$ g. $1\frac{2}{3}$ h. $1\frac{5}{9}$ j. $\frac{3}{5}$ k. NH

7. What fraction is another name for 29%?

  a. $\frac{29}{100}$ b. $\frac{29}{10}$ c. $\frac{29}{1000}$ d. $2\frac{2}{9}$ e. NH

---

3. What is the numeral for eleven thousand, four?

  a. 1,104
  b. 11,004
  c. 110,004
  d. 1,100,004
  e. NH

8. Which is a pair of prime numbers?

  f. (7, 54)
  g. (8, 13)
  h. (5, 18)
  j. (3, 19)
  k. NH

---

4. What is another way of writing 4^3?

  f. 4 x 4 x 4
  g. 14
  h. 4 + 4 + 4
  j. 4 x 3
  k. NH

9. Which number is between −6 and −1?

  a. −7
  b. −9
  c.   0
  d. −4
  e. NH

---

5. Solve for "n."
$\frac{1}{4} \times n = 0$

  a. 4   b. $\frac{4}{4}$ c. $\frac{3}{4}$ d. 0   e. NH

10. Which fraction names the smallest number?

  f. $\frac{2}{3}$ g. $\frac{3}{10}$ h. $\frac{4}{5}$ j. $\frac{1}{2}$ k. NH

Directions

Read each question and choose the correct answer. Mark the space for the answer you have chosen. Mark NH if the answer is not here.

---

1. What is 883.63 rounded to the nearest whole number?

   a. 884
   b. 883.6
   c. 880
   d. 900
   e. NH

6. Which is the greatest number?

   f. -12
   g. -7
   h. -3
   j. -1
   k. NH

---

2. Solve for "n."

$$3 \times (n + 6) = (3 \times 8) + (3 \times 6)$$

   f. 8
   g. 6
   h. 3
   j. 18
   k. NH

7. Which is a prime number?

   a. 9
   b. 17
   c. 21
   d. 27
   e. NH

---

3. What is the prime factorization of 20?

   a. 4 x 5
   b. 2 x 10
   c. 2 x 2 x 5
   d. 1 x 20
   e. NH

8. What is 487,084.68 rounded to the nearest hundred?

   f. 487,000
   g. 487,084.69
   h. 487,080
   j. 487,100
   k. NH

---

4. $5^2 =$

   f. 52
   g. 10
   h. 26
   j. 25
   k. NH

9. Which is another way of writing 3^4?

   a. 3 x 4
   b. 3 x 3 x 3 x 3
   c. 12 x 3
   d. 4 x 4 x 4
   e. NH

---

5. What fraction is another name for $\frac{1}{3}$?

   a. $\frac{2}{9}$ b. $\frac{1}{12}$ c. $\frac{4}{12}$ d. $\frac{2}{12}$ e. NH

10. What fraction is another name for 0.003?

   f. $\frac{3}{100}$ g. $\frac{3}{1,000}$ h. $\frac{3}{10}$ j. $\frac{3}{10,000}$ k. NH

Directions

Read each question and choose the correct answer. Mark the space for the answer you have chosen. Mark NH if the answer is not here.

---

1. What decimal is another name for $\frac{41}{100}$?

   a.   0.41
   b.   0.041
   c.   4.1
   d.   0.0041
   e.   NH

6. Which fraction is in its simplest form?

   f. $\frac{6}{15}$ g. $\frac{9}{21}$ h. $\frac{7}{12}$ j. $\frac{5}{20}$ k. NH

---

2. What fraction is another name for 0.36?

   f. $\frac{36}{10}$ g. $3\frac{3}{5}$ h. $\frac{12}{50}$ j. $\frac{9}{25}$ k. NH

7. What is the numeral for fifty-two thousand, five?

   a.   5,205
   b.   52,005
   c.   520,005
   d.   5,200,005
   e.   NH

---

3. $3^3 - 8 =$

   a.   19
   b.   1
   c.   25
   d.   17
   e.   NH

8. What number is 3 tenths more than 302.647?

   f.   302.947
   g.   332.647
   h.   305.647
   j.   302.677
   k.   NH

---

4. What is 189,753 rounded to the nearest hundred?

   f.   189,800
   g.   190,000
   h.   189,700
   j.   189,750
   k.   NH

9. What does the 7 in 3.75 represent?

   a. $\frac{7}{1}$ b. $\frac{7}{7}$ c. $\frac{7}{100}$ d. $\frac{7}{10}$ e. NH

---

5. What does the 2 in 123,047 represent?

   a.   2000
   b.   20,000
   c.   200,000
   d.   200
   e.   NH

10. What is the least common denominator for $\frac{1}{2}$, $\frac{3}{4}$, and $\frac{2}{5}$?

   f.   40
   g.   8
   h.   10
   j.   20
   k.   NH

Directions
Read each question and choose the correct answer. Mark the space for the answer you have chosen. Mark NH if the answer is not here.

---

1. What does the 3 in 4.230 represent?

   a. $\frac{3}{1}$ **b.** $\frac{3}{10}$ **c.** $\frac{3}{100}$ **d.** $\frac{3}{1,000}$ **e. NH**

6. What is the least common denominator for $\frac{1}{4}$, $\frac{1}{8}$, and $\frac{1}{3}$?

  f.   24
  g.   16
  h.   12
  j.   32
  k.   **NH**

---

2. What is the simplest form of $\frac{20}{7}$?

  f. 3   **g.** $2\frac{6}{7}$ **h.** $3\frac{1}{7}$ **j.** $2\frac{2}{7}$ **k. NH**

7. Which of the following is a prime number?

  a.   8
  b.   13
  c.   12
  d.   42
  e.   **NH**

---

3. What is the numeral for forty thousand, two?

  a.   402
  b.   40,002
  c.   4,002
  d.   42,000
  e.   **NH**

8. What is 29,856 rounded to the nearest hundred?

  f.   30,000
  g.   29,800
  h.   29,900
  j.   29,000
  k.   **NH**

---

4. What is 6.21 rounded to the nearest tenth?

  f.   6
  g.   6.3
  h.   6.2
  j.   7
  k.   **NH**

9. $4^3 =$

  a.   16
  b.   64
  c.   108
  d.   8
  e.   **NH**

---

5. Solve for "n."

  $(n \times 4) + 4 = (3 \times 4) = 12$

  a.   4
  b.   10
  c.   2
  d.   5
  e.   **NH**

10. Which is another way of writing $6 + (4 + 1)$?

  f. $(6 + 6) + (4 + 1)$
  g. $(6 + 4)$
  h. $(6 + 4) + 1$
  j. $(6 \times 4) + (4 \times 1)$
  k.   **NH**

Directions
Read each question and choose the correct answer. Mark the space for the answer you have chosen. Mark NH if the answer is not here.

---

1. What decimal is another name for 25%?

   a. 25.0
   b. 2.5
   c. 2.05
   d. 0.25
   e. NH

6. Which numbers are in order from least to greatest?

   f. $-6, -3, -2$
   g. $-3, -6, -2$
   h. $-2, -3, -6$
   j. $-3, -2, -6$
   k. NH

---

2. What does the 3 in 302,554 represent?

   f. 3,000
   g. 300,000
   h. 300
   j. 3
   k. NH

7. $3^3 + 7 =$

   a. 31
   b. 32
   c. 34
   d. 27
   e. NH

---

3. $12 + (-3) =$

   a. 9
   b. -9
   c. -15
   d. 15
   e. NH

8. Which is another name for 56?

   f. 8^2
   g. $8 + (24 \div 4)$
   h. $6 + (10 \times 5)$
   j. $15 + (2 \times 12)$
   k. NH

---

4. What fraction is another name for 0.09?

   f. $\frac{9}{10}$ g. $\frac{9}{100}$ h. $\frac{9}{1,000}$ j. $\frac{9}{10,000}$ k. NH

9. Which is a pair of prime numbers?

   a. (3, 36)
   b. (3, 11)
   c. (12, 38)
   d. (16, 4)
   e. NH

---

5. What is the numeral for twenty-one thousand, four hundred three?

   a. 2,143
   b. 240,304
   c. 24,103
   d. 21,403
   e. NH

10. What is 62,689 rounded to the nearest thousand?

   f. 62,700
   g. 62,690
   h. 63,000
   j. 63,790
   k. NH

Directions

Read each question and choose the correct answer. Mark the space for the answer you have chosen. Mark NH if the answer is not here.

1. 5 x 216 =

   a. 1,305
   b. 1,085
   c. 1,080
   d. 1,075
   e. NH

6. 879 x 137 =

   f. 284,349
   g. 155,181
   h. 122,889
   j. 120,423
   k. NH

2. 9 x 107 =

   f. 963
   g. 956
   h. 907
   j. 763
   k. NH

7. 514 x 63 =

   a. 34,083
   b. 32,382
   c. 19,476
   d. 18,504
   e. NH

3. 13 x 456 =

   a. 5,928
   b. 6,045
   c. 6,110
   d. 6,628
   e. NH

8. 8 x 269 =

   f. 1,738
   g. 1,792
   h. 2,152
   j. 2,368
   k. NH

4. 7 x 998 =

   f. 6,293
   g. 6,923
   h. 6,986
   j. 6,993
   k. NH

9. 29 x 37 =

   a. 1,073
   b. 1,131
   c. 2,113
   d. 6,716
   e. NH

5. 25 x 694 =

   a. 16,225
   b. 17,350
   c. 23,650
   d. 24,100
   e. NH

10. 359 x 559 =

   f. 199,461
   g. 199,245
   h. 200,681
   j. 215,041
   k. NH

Directions

Read each question and choose the correct answer. Mark the space for the answer you have chosen. Mark NH if the answer is not here.

---

1. 4,160 ÷ 5 =

   a. 805
   b. 812
   c. 823
   d. 832
   e. NH

6. 2,832 ÷ 59 =

   f. 48
   g. 57
   h. 62
   j. 68
   k. NH

---

2. 3,716 ÷ 4 =

   f. 919
   g. 922
   h. 929
   j. 934
   k. NH

7. 5,808 ÷ 12 =

   a. 440
   b. 448
   c. 454
   d. 484
   e. NH

---

3. 986 ÷ 58 =

   a. 17
   b. 19
   c. 24
   d. 32
   e. NH

8. 5,082 ÷ 6 =

   f. 847
   g. 849
   h. 856
   j. 857
   k. NH

---

4. 10,672 ÷ 92 =

   f. 107
   g. 116
   h. 120
   j. 147
   k. NH

9. 5,962 ÷ 22 =

   a. 246
   b. 267
   c. 271
   d. 279
   e. NH

---

5. 50,545 ÷ 55 =

   a. 919
   b. 927
   c. 930
   d. 945
   e. NH

10. 2,475 ÷ 3 =

   f. 65
   g. 72
   h. 75
   j. 105
   k. NH

Name _____

Directions

Read each question and choose the correct answer. Mark the space for the answer you have chosen. Mark NH if the answer is not here.

1. The quotient of 4,160 ÷ 5 is between which numbers?

    a. **10 and 20**
    b. **20 and 30**
    c. **30 and 40**
    d. **40 and 50**
    e. **NH**

2. The quotient of 625 ÷ 20 is between which numbers?

    f. **20 and 30**
    g. **30 and 40**
    h. **40 and 50**
    j. **50 and 60**
    k. **NH**

3. The quotient of 986 ÷ 58 is between which numbers?

    a. **90 and 100**
    b. **80 and 90**
    c. **70 and 80**
    d. **60 and 70**
    e. **NH**

4. The quotient of 887 ÷ 60 is between which numbers?

    f. **40 and 50**
    g. **30 and 40**
    h. **20 and 30**
    j. **10 and 20**
    k. **NH**

5. The quotient of 6,612 ÷ 70 is between which numbers?

    a. **70 and 80**
    b. **80 and 90**
    c. **90 and 100**
    d. **100 and 110**
    e. **NH**

6. The quotient of 6,150 ÷ 80 is between which numbers?

    f. **40 and 50**
    g. **50 and 60**
    h. **60 and 70**
    j. **70 and 80**
    k. **NH**

7. The quotient of 2,961 ÷ 70 is between which numbers?

    a. **20 and 30**
    b. **30 and 40**
    c. **40 and 50**
    d. **50 and 60**
    e. **NH**

8. The quotient of 3,791 ÷ 50 is between which numbers?

    f. **70 and 80**
    g. **60 and 70**
    h. **50 and 60**
    j. **40 and 50**
    k. **NH**

9. The quotient of 3,383 ÷ 90 is between which numbers?

    a. **20 and 30**
    b. **30 and 40**
    c. **40 and 50**
    d. **50 and 60**
    e. **NH**

10. The quotient of 5,920 ÷ 60 is between which numbers?

    f. **80 and 90**
    g. **90 and 100**
    h. **100 and 110**
    j. **110 and 120**
    k. **NH**

Name _____

Directions
Read each question and choose the correct answer. Mark the space for the answer you have chosen. Mark NH if the answer is not here.

---

1. 7.3 + 8.6 =

   a. 14.8
   b. 15.9
   c. 16.8
   d. 16.9
   e. NH

6. $36.24 + $41.23 =

   f. $70.47
   g. $74.47
   h. $77.47
   j. $77.74
   k. NH

---

2. 6 + 2.3 =

   f. 2.9
   g. 8.3
   h. 8.9
   j. 9.3
   k. NH

7. 5.26 + 3.3 + 4 =

   a. 8.6
   b. 12.56
   c. 5.63
   d. 5.96
   e. NH

---

3. $13.59 + $16.40

   a. $29.36
   b. $29.63
   c. $29.99
   d. $39.36
   e. NH

8. 3.2 + 4.39 =

   f. 4.71
   g. 7.59
   h. 7.91
   j. 7.95
   k. NH

---

4. 23.5 + 16.5 =

   f. 40.0
   g. 4.00
   h. 29.0
   j. 13.0
   k. NH

9. $161.59 + $352.19 =

   a. $503.38
   b. $511.78
   c. $513.78
   d. $533.87
   e. NH

---

5. $7.25 + $1.31 =

   a. $8.83
   b. $8.76
   c. $8.65
   d. $8.56
   e. NH

10. $68.49 + $234.18 =

   f. $302.67
   g. $512.57
   h. $708.31
   j. $919.08
   k. NH

Directions
Read each question and choose the correct answer. Mark the space for the answer you have chosen. Mark NH if the answer is not here.

1. 8.4 − 2.7 =

   a. 5.7
   b. 6.3
   c. 6.7
   d. 6.8
   e. NH

6. 63.25 − 6.1 =

   f. 56.94
   g. 57.10
   h. 57.14
   j. 57.15
   k. NH

2. $15 − $3.96 =

   f. $11.04
   g. $10.96
   h. $12.96
   j. $10.04
   k. NH

7. 3.08 − 1.886 =

   a. 2.806
   b. 1.194
   c. 1.086
   d. 1.084
   e. NH

3. 4.3 − 1.22 =

   a. 3.08
   b. 3.12
   c. 3.99
   d. 4.21
   e. NH

8. $302 − $287.41 =

   f. $14.59
   g. $14.95
   h. $15.49
   j. $15.59
   k. NH

4. 63.25 − 58.269 =

   f. 5.639
   g. 5.031
   h. 4.999
   j. 4.981
   k. NH

9. 7.2 − 6.51 =

   a. 1.39
   b. 1.31
   c. 0.71
   d. 0.69
   e. NH

5. 5.21 − 2.6 =

   a. 2.16
   b. 2.26
   c. 2.6
   d. 2.61
   e. NH

10. 15.02 − 9.3 =

   f. 6.99
   g. 5.89
   h. 5.82
   j. 5.72
   k. NH

Name _____

Directions
Read each question and choose the correct answer. Mark the space for the answer you have chosen. Mark NH if the answer is not here.

1. 5 x 17.2 =

   a. 8.6
   b. 85.10
   c. 86.0
   d. 86.1
   e. NH

2. 110 x 6.5 =

   f. 715.0
   g. 710.5
   h. 705.10
   j. 71.5
   k. NH

3. 0.15 x 0.5 =

   a. 0.075
   b. 0.75
   c. 7.5
   d. 75.0
   e. NH

4. 2.5 x 3.2 =

   f. 80.0
   g. 8.0
   h. 800.0
   j. 8.02
   k. NH

5. 0.601 x 2 =

   a. 12.01
   b. 1.202
   c. 0.12
   d. 1.2
   e. NH

6. 215.3 x 7 =

   f. 1,501.41
   g. 1,504.1
   h. 1,505.21
   j. 1,507.1
   k. NH

7. 5.6 x 0.7 =

   a. 39.2
   b. 3.092
   c. 0.392
   d. 0.0392
   e. NH

8. 1.25 x 0.8 =

   f. 10.0
   g. 1.0
   h. 0.1
   j. 0.01
   k. NH

9. 3.6 x 2.5 =

   a. 9
   b. 8.8
   c. 32.65
   d. 9.3
   e. NH

10. 4.5 x 30 =

   f. 1.35
   g. 1.035
   h. 13.5
   j. 135.0
   k. NH

Name _____

Directions
Read each question and choose the correct answer. Mark the space for the answer you have chosen. Mark NH if the answer is not here.

1. 27.2 ÷ 4 =

   a. 680
   b. 68
   c. 6.8
   d. 0.68
   e. NH

6. 1.008 ÷ 0.2 =

   f. 5.4
   g. 50.4
   h. 50.04
   j. 5.04
   k. NH

2. 83.5 ÷ 0.5 =

   f. 167
   g. 16.7
   h. 1.67
   j. 0.167
   k. NH

7. 6.25 ÷ 5 =

   a. 1.25
   b. 12.5
   c. 125
   d. 1,250
   e. NH

3. 96 ÷ 1.2 =

   a. 800
   b. 80
   c. 8
   d. 0.8
   e. NH

8. 7.02 ÷ 0.2 =

   f. 0.351
   g. 3.51
   h. 35.1
   j. 351
   k. NH

4. 62.35 ÷ 5 =

   f. 1.247
   g. 12.47
   h. 124.7
   j. 1247
   k. NH

9. 36.777 ÷ 7.995 =

   a. 0.46
   b. 46
   c. 4.6
   d. 460
   e. NH

5. 336 ÷ 0.4 =

   a. 0.84
   b. 8.4
   c. 84
   d. 840
   e. NH

10. 9.5 ÷ 0.19 =

   f. 0.5
   g. 0.05
   h. 5.0
   j. 500
   k. NH

Name _____

Directions
Read each question and choose the correct answer. Mark the space for the answer you have chosen. Mark NH if the answer is not here.

---

1. Estimate the answer by rounding:
45.36 ÷ 8.9

   a. 2
   b. 3
   c. 4
   d. 5
   e. NH

6. Estimate the answer by rounding:
46.84 ÷ 8.17

   f. 4
   g. 5
   h. 6
   j. 7
   k. NH

---

2. Estimate the answer by rounding:
27.961 ÷ 4.13

   f. 5
   g. 6
   h. 7
   j. 8
   k. NH

7. Estimate the answer by rounding:
61.264 ÷ 7.26

   a. 6
   b. 7
   c. 10
   d. 9
   e. NH

---

3. Estimate the answer by rounding:
56.002 ÷ 9.99

   a. 5
   b. 6
   c. 7
   d. 8
   e. NH

8. Estimate the answer by rounding:
95.74 ÷ 11.63

   f. 9
   g. 8
   h. 7
   j. 6
   k. NH

---

4. Estimate the answer by rounding:
71.5 ÷ 11.667

   f. 5
   g. 6
   h. 7
   j. 8
   k. NH

9. Estimate the answer by rounding:
143.872 ÷ 12.02

   a. 10
   b. 11
   c. 12
   d. 13
   e. NH

---

5. Estimate the answer by rounding:
24.398 ÷ 7.6

   a. 5
   b. 4
   c. 3
   d. 2
   e. NH

10. Estimate the answer by rounding:
99.42 ÷ 9.9

   f. 7
   g. 8
   h. 9
   j. 10
   k. NH

Directions

Read each question and choose the correct answer. Mark the space for the answer you have chosen. Mark NH if the answer is not here.

1. $\frac{3}{8} + \frac{5}{8} =$

    a. $1\frac{7}{8}$ d. 1

    b. $\frac{2}{16}$ e. NH

    c. $\frac{8}{16}$

6. $\frac{1}{2} + \frac{3}{8} =$

    f. $7\frac{1}{8}$ j. $8\frac{7}{8}$

    g. $7\frac{7}{8}$ k. NH

    h. $8\frac{1}{8}$

2. $\frac{1}{3} + \frac{1}{2} =$

    f. $5\frac{5}{6}$ j. $4\frac{5}{6}$

    g. $5\frac{1}{6}$ k. NH

    h. $4\frac{1}{6}$

7. $\frac{2}{3} + \frac{4}{9} =$

    a. $1\frac{1}{9}$ d. $\frac{8}{9}$

    b. $1\frac{2}{9}$ e. NH

    c. $\frac{7}{9}$

3. $\frac{2}{5} + \frac{1}{3} =$

    a. $\frac{11}{15}$ d. $\frac{1}{5}$

    b. $\frac{3}{8}$ e. NH

    c. $\frac{3}{15}$

8. $\frac{5}{6} + \frac{5}{9} =$

    f. $10\frac{1}{2}$ j. $1\frac{2}{18}$

    g. $1\frac{1}{2}$ k. NH

    h. $1\frac{5}{18}$

4. $\frac{5}{12} + \frac{1}{6} =$

    f. $\frac{6}{12}$ j. $\frac{7}{12}$

    g. $\frac{2}{12}$ k. NH

    h. $\frac{5}{12}$

9. $\frac{2}{5} + \frac{3}{10} =$

    a. $12\frac{5}{15}$ d. $13\frac{7}{10}$

    b. $12\frac{1}{3}$ e. NH

    c. $12\frac{6}{10}$

5. $\frac{2}{3} + \frac{1}{4} =$

    a. $9\frac{9}{12}$ d. $10\frac{11}{12}$

    b. $9\frac{11}{12}$ e. NH

    c. $10\frac{1}{12}$

10. $\frac{1}{3} + \frac{5}{7} =$

    f. $\frac{3}{7}$ j. $\frac{3}{5}$

    g. $\frac{20}{21}$ k. NH

    h. $1\frac{1}{21}$

Name _____ Skill: Subtraction of Fractions and Mixed Numbers

Directions
Read each question and choose the correct answer. Mark the space for the answer you have chosen. Mark NH if the answer is not here.

1. $\frac{4}{5} - \frac{2}{3} =$

   a. $\frac{1}{15}$ d. $\frac{4}{15}$

   b. $\frac{2}{15}$ e. NH

   c. $\frac{1}{5}$

2. $5\frac{3}{4} - 2\frac{1}{3} =$

   f. $3\frac{2}{3}$ j. $3\frac{1}{3}$

   g. $3\frac{1}{2}$ k. NH

   h. $3\frac{5}{12}$

3. $3 - 1\frac{1}{3} =$

   a. $1\frac{1}{3}$ d. $1\frac{2}{3}$

   b. $2\frac{1}{3}$ e. NH

   c. $2\frac{2}{3}$

4. $\frac{3}{5} - \frac{1}{2} =$

   f. $\frac{1}{10}$ j. $\frac{1}{2}$

   g. $\frac{1}{5}$ k. NH

   h. $\frac{1}{3}$

5. $8\frac{1}{2} - 4\frac{4}{9} =$

   a. $4\frac{1}{9}$ d. $3\frac{5}{6}$

   b. $4\frac{1}{18}$ e. NH

   c. $3\frac{17}{18}$

6. $7\frac{1}{3} - \frac{5}{9} =$

   f. $6\frac{1}{3}$ j. $6\frac{5}{9}$

   g. $5\frac{7}{9}$ k. NH

   h. $6\frac{7}{9}$

7. $3\frac{3}{4} - 2\frac{1}{8} =$

   a. $1\frac{1}{4}$ d. $1\frac{2}{3}$

   b. $1\frac{7}{8}$ e. NH

   c. $1\frac{5}{8}$

8. $\frac{8}{9} - \frac{2}{3} =$

   f. 1 j. $\frac{2}{9}$

   g. $\frac{1}{9}$ k. NH

   h. $\frac{1}{3}$

9. $4\frac{1}{5} - 1\frac{1}{2} =$

   a. $2\frac{7}{10}$ d. $2\frac{3}{5}$

   b. $3\frac{3}{10}$ e. NH

   c. $2\frac{1}{2}$

10. $6 - 5\frac{1}{4} =$

   f. $\frac{1}{4}$ j. $1\frac{1}{4}$

   g. $\frac{1}{2}$ k. NH

   h. $\frac{3}{4}$

Directions
Read each question and choose the correct answer. Mark the space for the answer you have chosen. Mark NH if the answer is not here.

1. $\frac{2}{3}$ x $\frac{6}{5}$ =

    a. $\frac{5}{6}$ **d.** $\frac{4}{5}$

    b. $\frac{2}{3}$ **e.** NH

    c. $\frac{1}{2}$

6. $\frac{7}{8}$ x $\frac{4}{5}$ =

    f. $\frac{4}{5}$ **j.** $\frac{7}{10}$

    g. $\frac{8}{9}$ **k.** NH

    h. $\frac{3}{5}$

2. $\frac{1}{2}$ x $\frac{4}{5}$ =

    f. 15   **j.** $\frac{4}{7}$

    g. $\frac{2}{5}$ **k.** NH

    h. $\frac{4}{5}$

7. $\frac{6}{7}$ x $\frac{2}{3}$ =

    a. $\frac{4}{7}$ **d.** $\frac{8}{10}$

    b. $\frac{1}{2}$ **e.** NH

    c. $\frac{3}{4}$

3. $\frac{3}{4}$ x $\frac{5}{6}$ =

    a. $\frac{5}{6}$ **d.** $\frac{7}{8}$

    b. $\frac{2}{3}$ **e.** NH

    c. $\frac{5}{8}$

8. $\frac{2}{9}$ x $\frac{3}{4}$ =

    f. $\frac{1}{5}$ **j.** $\frac{1}{2}$

    g. $\frac{3}{5}$ **k.** NH

    h. $\frac{1}{6}$

4. $\frac{1}{3}$ x $\frac{2}{3}$ =

    f. $\frac{1}{2}$ **j.** $\frac{2}{9}$

    g. $\frac{1}{3}$ **k.** NH

    h. $\frac{2}{6}$

9. $\frac{5}{8}$ x $\frac{5}{10}$ =

    a. $\frac{1}{2}$ **d.** $\frac{7}{8}$

    b. $\frac{5}{16}$ **e.** NH

    c. $\frac{3}{4}$

5. $\frac{4}{5}$ x $\frac{10}{11}$ =

    a. $\frac{8}{11}$ **d.** $\frac{6}{11}$

    b. $\frac{5}{9}$ **e.** NH

    c. $\frac{4}{9}$

10. $\frac{2}{3}$ x $\frac{1}{4}$ =

    f. $\frac{1}{2}$ **j.** $\frac{1}{6}$

    g. $\frac{2}{3}$ **k.** NH

    h. $\frac{1}{3}$

Directions
Read each question and choose the correct answer. Mark the space for the answer you have chosen. Mark NH if the answer is not here.

---

1. $1\frac{1}{2} \times \frac{1}{3} =$

    a. $\frac{1}{3}$ **d.** $\frac{5}{6}$

    b. $\frac{1}{2}$ **e.** NH

    c. 1

6. $7\frac{1}{2} \times 1\frac{3}{5} =$

    f. $7\frac{3}{10}$ **j.** 15

    g. 7   **k.** NH

    h. 12

---

2. $1\frac{3}{4} \times \frac{2}{7} =$

    f. $\frac{1}{2}$ **j.** $\frac{1}{7}$

    g. $\frac{1}{4}$ **k.** NH

    h. $\frac{2}{7}$

7. $4\frac{2}{3} \times \frac{3}{7} =$

    a. $4\frac{2}{7}$ **d.** $2\frac{1}{2}$

    b. $4\frac{1}{3}$ **e.** NH

    c. 2

---

3. $\frac{5}{6} \times 2\frac{2}{5} =$

    a. 1   **d.** $2\frac{1}{2}$

    b. $1\frac{1}{2}$ **e.** NH

    c. 2

8. $1\frac{2}{3} \times \frac{3}{5} =$

    f. $1\frac{2}{5}$ **j.** $2\frac{2}{3}$

    g. $1\frac{1}{2}$ **k.** NH

    h. 1

---

4. $2\frac{2}{3} \times 1\frac{1}{2} =$

    f. $2\frac{1}{3}$ **j.** 4

    g. $2\frac{1}{2}$ **k.** NH

    h. $3\frac{3}{4}$

9. $2\frac{2}{3} \times \frac{1}{4} =$

    a. $\frac{2}{3}$ **d.** $2\frac{3}{3}$

    b. $1\frac{1}{3}$ **e.** NH

    c. $2\frac{1}{3}$

---

5. $1\frac{7}{8} \times \frac{2}{5} =$

    a. $\frac{2}{3}$ **d.** $\frac{3}{5}$

    b. $\frac{2}{5}$ **e.** NH

    c. $\frac{3}{4}$

10. $5\frac{1}{4} \times \frac{4}{7} =$

    f. $5\frac{1}{7}$ **j.** 3

    g. $4\frac{1}{2}$ **k.** NH

    h. $3\frac{2}{3}$

Directions
Read each question and choose the correct answer. Mark the space for the answer you have chosen. Mark NH if the answer is not here.

---

1. $\frac{1}{4} \div \frac{1}{2} =$

   a. $\frac{1}{3}$ **d.** 2

   b. $\frac{1}{2}$ **e.** NH

   c. $\frac{1}{8}$

6. $\frac{1}{2} \div \frac{2}{3} =$

   f. $\frac{3}{4}$ **j.** $1\frac{1}{3}$

   g. $\frac{1}{3}$ **k.** NH

   h. $\frac{1}{2}$

---

2. $\frac{4}{5} \div \frac{2}{3} =$

   f. $1\frac{1}{5}$ **j.** $\frac{10}{12}$

   g. $\frac{5}{6}$ **k.** NH

   h. $\frac{8}{15}$

7. $\frac{3}{5} \div \frac{1}{2} =$

   a. $\frac{5}{6}$ **d.** $\frac{3}{10}$

   b. $1\frac{1}{5}$ **e.** NH

   c. $\frac{3}{4}$

---

3. $\frac{1}{6} \div \frac{1}{3} =$

   a. $\frac{1}{18}$ **d.** $\frac{1}{2}$

   b. $\frac{1}{3}$ **e.** NH

   c. 2

8. $\frac{5}{6} \div \frac{2}{3} =$

   f. $\frac{4}{5}$ **j.** $\frac{4}{2}$

   g. $1\frac{1}{4}$ **k.** NH

   h. $\frac{5}{9}$

---

4. $\frac{3}{4} \div \frac{1}{3} =$

   f. $\frac{1}{4}$ **j.** $\frac{5}{6}$

   g. $2\frac{1}{4}$ **k.** NH

   h. $1\frac{1}{4}$

9. $\frac{1}{4} \div \frac{1}{3} =$

   a. $\frac{1}{12}$ **d.** $\frac{3}{4}$

   b. $1\frac{1}{3}$ **e.** NH

   c. $\frac{1}{2}$

---

5. $\frac{2}{5} \div \frac{2}{3} =$

   a. $\frac{4}{15}$ **d.** $\frac{4}{9}$

   b. $1\frac{2}{3}$ **e.** NH

   c. $\frac{3}{5}$

10. $\frac{2}{3} \div \frac{1}{4} =$

   f. $2\frac{2}{3}$ **j.** $2\frac{3}{3}$

   g. $1\frac{1}{3}$ **k.** NH

   h. $2\frac{1}{3}$

Name _____

Directions

Read each question and choose the correct answer. Mark the space for the answer you have chosen. Mark NH if the answer is not here.

1. $1\frac{1}{2} \div 3 =$

a. 2   d. $\frac{2}{3}$

b. 6   e. NH

c. $\frac{1}{2}$

2. $\frac{7}{8} \div 1\frac{1}{3} =$

f. $\frac{5}{8}$ j. $\frac{21}{32}$

g. $\frac{1}{7}$ k. NH

h. $\frac{1}{16}$

3. $\frac{5}{6} \div 1\frac{1}{2} =$

a. $1\frac{4}{5}$ d. $1\frac{1}{2}$

b. $\frac{5}{9}$ e. NH

c. $\frac{5}{6}$

4. $5\frac{1}{3} \div 1\frac{2}{9} =$

f. $\frac{11}{48}$ j. $\frac{9}{10}$

g. $4\frac{4}{11}$ k. NH

h. $\frac{7}{8}$

5. $5\frac{1}{5} \div 1\frac{3}{10} =$

a. $\frac{1}{4}$ d. 4

b. $\frac{5}{7}$ e. NH

c. $3\frac{1}{2}$

6. $4\frac{1}{2} \div 1\frac{1}{2} =$

f. 2   j. 3

g. $2\frac{1}{2}$ k. NH

h. $\frac{1}{3}$

7. $7\frac{1}{2} \div 3 =$

a. $\frac{2}{5}$ d. $2\frac{1}{2}$

b. $\frac{3}{7}$ e. NH

c. $\frac{4}{7}$

8. $3\frac{3}{4} \div \frac{5}{6} =$

f. $\frac{2}{9}$ j. $3\frac{1}{8}$

g. $4\frac{1}{2}$ k. NH

h. $3\frac{1}{3}$

9. $2\frac{1}{3} \div \frac{7}{8} =$

a. $\frac{3}{8}$ d. $1\frac{7}{8}$

b. $\frac{4}{5}$ e. NH

c. $2\frac{2}{3}$

10. $2\frac{3}{4} \div 3\frac{2}{3} =$

f. $2\frac{7}{10}$ j. $2\frac{3}{5}$

g. $\frac{3}{10}$ k. NH

h. $\frac{3}{4}$

Name _____

Directions
Read each question and choose the correct answer. Mark the space for the answer you have chosen. Mark NH if the answer is not here.

1. 9% of 200 =

a. 1.8
b. 180
c. 0.18
d. 18
e. NH

2. 2% of 200 =

f. 40
g. 4
h. 0.4
j. .04
k. NH

3. 11% of 300 =

a. 30
b. 3.3
c. 1.3
d. .33
e. NH

4. 5% of 600 =

f. 3
g. 30
h. 300
j. 6.5
k. NH

5. 12% of 800 =

a. 9.6
b. 96
c. 128
d. 0.96
e. NH

6. 4% of 400 =

f. 44
g. 1.6
h. 16
j. 160
k. NH

7. 12% of 100 =

a. 1.2
b. 0.12
c. 12
d. 120
e. NH

8. 3% of 900 =

f. 27
g. 2.7
h. 0.27
j. 270
k. NH

9. 10% of 250 =

a. 2.5
b. 25
c. 250
d. 0.25
e. NH

10. 5% of 220 =

f. 1.1
g. 100
h. 110
j. 11
k. NH

Directions
Read each question and choose the correct answer. Mark the space for the answer you have chosen. Mark NH if the answer is not here.

1. 5 is 10% of what number?

a. 5
b. 25
c. 500
d. 50
e. NH

2. 12 is 20% of what number?

f. 120
g. 240
h. 1,200
j. 60
k. NH

3. 9 is 30% of what number?

a. 90
b. 30
c. 300
d. 3
e. NH

4. 4 is 5% of what number?

f. 80
g. 8
h. 800
j. 20
k. NH

5. 6 is 12% of what number?

a. 72
b. 500
c. 50
d. 5
e. NH

6. 11 is 20% of what number?

f. 50
g. 55
h. 22
j. 20
k. NH

7. 3 is 50% of what number?

a. 6
b. 60
c. 15
d. 1.5
e. NH

8. 8 is 40% of what number?

f. 20
g. 32
h. 320
j. 200
k. NH

9. 22 is 20% of what number?

a. 44
b. 440
c. 110
d. 11
e. NH

10. 81 is 30% of what number?

f. 27
g. 270
h. 30
j. 300
k. NH

Directions
Read each question and choose the correct answer. Mark the space for the answer you have chosen. Mark NH if the answer is not here.

1. 6 is what percent of 20?

    a. 10%
    b. 20%
    c. 30%
    d. 40%
    e. NH

6. 12 is what percent of 48?

    f. 25%
    g. 30%
    h. 40%
    j. 45%
    k. NH

2. 9 is what percent of 18?

    f. 25%
    g. 50%
    h. 75%
    j. 90%
    k. NH

7. 4 is what percent of 40?

    a. 5%
    b. 10%
    c. 20%
    d. 50%
    e. NH

3. 10 is what percent of 50?

    a. 20%
    b. 25%
    c. 40%
    d. 50%
    e. NH

8. 8 is what percent of 32?

    f. 20%
    g. 25%
    h. 30%
    j. 50%
    k. NH

4. 15 is what percent of 30?

    f. 50%
    g. 60%
    h. 70%
    j. 75%
    k. NH

9. 5 is what percent of 25?

    a. 10%
    b. 15%
    c. 18%
    d. 20%
    e. NH

5. 16 is what percent of 20?

    a. 75%
    b. 80%
    c. 90%
    d. 95%
    e. NH

10. 100 is what percent of 500?

    f. 10%
    g. 20%
    h. 25%
    j. 50%
    k. NH

Directions

Read each question and choose the correct answer. Mark the space for the answer you have chosen. Mark NH if the answer is not here.

1. If $n + 2 = 7$, then $n =$

    a. 3
    b. 4
    c. 5
    d. 6
    e. NH

6. If $n + 9 = 15$, then $n =$

    f. 8
    g. 7
    h. 6
    j. 5
    k. NH

2. If $n + 3 = 9$, then $n =$

    f. 6
    g. 5
    h. 4
    j. 3
    k. NH

7. If $n + 3 = 7$, then $n =$

    a. 7
    b. 6
    c. 5
    d. 4
    e. NH

3. If $n + 7 = 9$, then $n =$

    a. 4
    b. 3
    c. 2
    d. 1
    e. NH

8. If $n + 5 = 11$, then $n =$

    f. 9
    g. 8
    h. 7
    j. 6
    k. NH

4. If $n + 4 = 8$, then $n =$

    f. 3
    g. 4
    h. 5
    j. 6
    k. NH

9. If $n + 7 = 13$, then $n =$

    a. 8
    b. 7
    c. 6
    d. 5
    e. NH

5. If $n + 3 = 12$, then $n =$

    a. 6
    b. 7
    c. 8
    d. 9
    e. NH

10. If $n + 5 = 13$, then $n =$

    f. 7
    g. 8
    h. 9
    j. 10
    k. NH

Directions

Read each question and choose the correct answer. Mark the space for the answer you have chosen. Mark NH if the answer is not here.

---

1. If $n - 2 = 4$, then $n =$

   a. 9
   b. 8
   c. 7
   d. 6
   e. NH

6. If $n - 5 = 9$, then $n =$

   f. 14
   g. 13
   h. 12
   j. 11
   k. NH

---

2. If $n - 6 = 8$, then $n =$

   f. 12
   g. 13
   h. 14
   j. 15
   k. NH

7. If $n - 9 = 7$, then $n =$

   a. 17
   b. 16
   c. 15
   d. 14
   e. NH

---

3. If $n - 5 = 2$, then $n =$

   a. 5
   b. 6
   c. 7
   d. 8
   e. NH

8. If $n - 4 = 7$, then $n =$

   f. 8
   g. 9
   h. 10
   j. 11
   k. NH

---

4. If $n - 4 = 1$, then $n =$

   f. 4
   g. 5
   h. 6
   j. 7
   k. NH

9. If $n - 6 = 3$, then $n =$

   a. 8
   b. 9
   c. 10
   d. 11
   e. NH

---

5. If $n - 8 = 3$, then $n =$

   a. 8
   b. 9
   c. 10
   d. 11
   e. NH

10. If $n - 4 = 8$, then $n =$

   f. 12
   g. 13
   h. 14
   j. 15
   k. NH

Directions

Read each question and choose the correct answer. Mark the space for the answer you have chosen. Mark NH if the answer is not here.

1. If 2n = 8, then n =

   a. 10
   b. 8
   c. 6
   d. 4
   e. NH

6. If 4y = 28, then y =

   f. 6
   g. 7
   h. 8
   j. 9
   k. NH

2. If 5n = 15, then n =

   f. 5
   g. 3
   h. 18
   j. 20
   k. NH

7. If 3y = 36, then y =

   a. 9
   b. 10
   c. 11
   d. 12
   e. NH

3. If 3n = 21, then n =

   a. 6
   b. 7
   c. 8
   d. 9
   e. NH

8. If 6y = 48, then y =

   f. 9
   g. 8
   h. 7
   j. 6
   k. NH

4. If 6n = 36, then n =

   f. 24
   g. 18
   h. 12
   j. 6
   k. NH

9. If 9y = 27, then y =

   a. 5
   b. 4
   c. 3
   d. 2
   e. NH

5. If 10n = 50, then n =

   a. 5
   b. 10
   c. 15
   d. 20
   e. NH

10. If 6y = 42, then y =

   f. 10
   g. 9
   h. 8
   j. 7
   k. NH

Directions

Read each question and choose the correct answer. Mark the space for the answer you have chosen. Mark NH if the answer is not here.

1. If $\frac{n}{3}$ = 6, then n =

   a. 2
   b. 9
   c. 18
   d. 27
   e. NH

6. If $\frac{n}{3}$ = 11, then n =

   f. 27
   g. 30
   h. 33
   j. 36
   k. NH

2. If $\frac{n}{8}$ = 8, then n =

   f. 1
   g. 16
   h. 32
   j. 64
   k. NH

7. If $\frac{n}{8}$ = 4, then n =

   a. 12
   b. 16
   c. 24
   d. 32
   e. NH

3. If $\frac{n}{2}$ = 6, then n =

   a. 3
   b. 12
   c. 18
   d. 24
   e. NH

8. If $\frac{n}{4}$ = 9, then n =

   f. 13
   g. 16
   h. 18
   j. 36
   k. NH

4. If $\frac{n}{5}$ = 3, then n =

   f. 5
   g. 10
   h. 15
   j. 20
   k. NH

9. If $\frac{n}{6}$ = 7, then n =

   a. 49
   b. 42
   c. 24
   d. 13
   e. NH

5. If $\frac{n}{6}$ = 2, then n =

   a. 12
   b. 18
   c. 72
   d. 144
   e. NH

10. If $\frac{n}{3}$ = 9, then n =

   f. 27
   g. 24
   h. 18
   j. 12
   k. NH

Name _____

Directions

Read each question and choose the correct answer. Mark the space for the answer you have chosen. Mark NH if the answer is not here.

1. If n = 3, then 2n + 5 =

   a. 9
   b. 10
   c. 11
   d. 12
   e. NH

2. If n = 7, then 3n − 4 =

   f. 14
   g. 15
   h. 16
   j. 17
   k. NH

3. If n = 2, then 8n + 3 =

   a. 13
   b. 12
   c. 11
   d. 10
   e. NH

4. If n = 5, then 4n + 6 =

   f. 24
   g. 25
   h. 26
   j. 27
   k. NH

5. If n = 4, then 2n + 7 =

   a. 14
   b. 15
   c. 16
   d. 17
   e. NH

6. If n = 12, then 2n − 1 =

   f. 20
   g. 21
   h. 22
   j. 23
   k. NH

7. If n = 9, then 3n + 4 =

   a. 28
   b. 29
   c. 30
   d. 31
   e. NH

8. If n = 4, then 3n − 2 =

   f. 8
   g. 9
   h. 10
   j. 11
   k. NH

9. If n = 7, then 2n + 6 =

   a. 20
   b. 19
   c. 18
   d. 17
   e. NH

10. If n = 5, then 3n + 8 =

   f. 22
   g. 23
   h. 24
   j. 25
   k. NH

Directions

Read each question and choose the correct answer. Mark the space for the answer you have chosen. Mark NH if the answer is not here.

1. If n = 2, then 10n + 6 =

   a. 23
   b. 24
   c. 25
   d. 26
   e. NH

6. If n = 11, then 4n + 8 =

   f. 51
   g. 52
   h. 53
   j. 54
   k. NH

2. If n = 8, then 7n − 2 =

   f. 51
   g. 52
   h. 53
   j. 54
   k. NH

7. If n = 6, then 10n − 4 =

   a. 54
   b. 55
   c. 56
   d. 57
   e. NH

3. If n = 7, then 6n + 5 =

   a. 44
   b. 45
   c. 46
   d. 47
   e. NH

8. If n = 8, then 6n + 9 =

   f. 55
   g. 56
   h. 57
   j. 58
   k. NH

4. If n = 3, then 12n + 6 =

   f. 40
   g. 41
   h. 42
   j. 43
   k. NH

9. If n = 5, then 11n + 4 =

   a. 58
   b. 59
   c. 60
   d. 61
   e. NH

5. If n = 5, then 12n − 7 =

   a. 52
   b. 53
   c. 54
   d. 55
   e. NH

10. If n = 7, then 8n − 4 =

   f. 58
   g. 59
   h. 61
   j. 62
   k. NH

Name _____

Directions

Read each question and choose the correct answer. Mark the space for the answer you have chosen. Mark NH if the answer is not here.

---

1. If $\frac{2}{3} = \frac{n}{9}$, then n =

    a. 2
    b. 4
    c. 6
    d. 8
    e. NH

6. If $\frac{3}{4} = \frac{n}{28}$, then n =

    f. 15
    g. 18
    h. 21
    j. 24
    k. NH

---

2. If $\frac{3}{5} = \frac{12}{n}$, then n =

    f. 10
    g. 15
    h. 20
    j. 25
    k. NH

7. If $\frac{2}{4} = \frac{6}{n}$, then n =

    a. 8
    b. 10
    c. 12
    d. 14
    e. NH

---

3. If $\frac{7}{8} = \frac{n}{16}$, then n =

    a. 1
    b. 2
    c. 12
    d. 14
    e. NH

8. If $\frac{1}{3} = \frac{n}{15}$, then n =

    f. 5
    g. 6
    h. 7
    j. 8
    k. NH

---

4. If $\frac{2}{5} = \frac{n}{30}$, then n =

    f. 12
    g. 14
    h. 16
    j. 18
    k. NH

9. If $\frac{2}{3} = \frac{14}{n}$, then n =

    a. 16
    b. 18
    c. 21
    d. 24
    e. NH

---

5. If $\frac{4}{7} = \frac{n}{21}$, then n =

    a. 3
    b. 6
    c. 12
    d. 18
    e. NH

10. If $\frac{6}{7} = \frac{n}{28}$, then n =

    f. 12
    g. 18
    h. 24
    j. 36
    k. NH

Directions

Read each question and choose the correct answer. Mark the space for the answer you have chosen. Mark NH if the answer is not here.

1. If $\frac{6}{9} = \frac{n}{12}$, then n =

    a. 4
    b. 6
    c. 8
    d. 10
    e. NH

6. If $\frac{6}{12} = \frac{10}{n}$, then n =

    f. 9
    g. 10
    h. 12
    j. 20
    k. NH

2. If $\frac{6}{8} = \frac{15}{n}$, then n =

    f. 20
    g. 24
    h. 28
    j. 32
    k. NH

7. If $\frac{12}{16} = \frac{n}{12}$, then n =

    a. 9
    b. 12
    c. 15
    d. 18
    e. NH

3. If $\frac{6}{10} = \frac{n}{15}$, then n =

    a. 6
    b. 9
    c. 12
    d. 15
    e. NH

8. If $\frac{6}{15} = \frac{4}{n}$, then n =

    f. 8
    g. 10
    h. 12
    j. 16
    k. NH

4. If $\frac{2}{4} = \frac{n}{10}$, then n =

    f. 4
    g. 5
    h. 6
    j. 7
    k. NH

9. If $\frac{3}{12} = \frac{n}{8}$, then n =

    a. 2
    b. 4
    c. 6
    d. 8
    e. NH

5. If $\frac{4}{8} = \frac{9}{n}$, then n =

    a. 16
    b. 18
    c. 20
    d. 22
    e. NH

10. If $\frac{6}{8} = \frac{n}{24}$, then n =

    f. 14
    g. 16
    h. 18
    j. 20
    k. NH

Directions

Read each question and choose the correct answer. Mark the space for the answer you have chosen. Mark NH if the answer is not here.

1. Which is the subset of the solution set for the inequality 2y < 16?

   a. {2, 4, 6}
   b. {4, 6, 8}
   c. {6, 8, 10}
   d. {10, 12, 14}
   e. NH

6. Which is the subset of the solution set for the inequality 4y > 36?

   f. {6, 8, 10}
   g. {10, 12, 14}
   h. {7, 8, 9}
   j. {6, 8, 10}
   k. NH

2. Which is the subset of the solution set for the inequality 3y > 18?

   f. {3, 4, 5}
   g. {5, 6, 7}
   h. {7, 8, 9}
   j. {6, 9, 12}
   k. NH

7. Which is the subset of the solution set for the inequality 3y > 15?

   a. {6, 8, 10}
   b. {4, 5, 6}
   c. {1, 3, 5}
   d. {2, 4, 6}
   e. NH

3. Which is the subset of the solution set for the inequality 5y > 20?

   a. {1, 2, 3}
   b. {2, 3, 4}
   c. {4, 5, 6}
   d. {5, 6, 7}
   e. NH

8. Which is the subset of the solution set for the inequality 5y < 30?

   f. {2, 3, 5}
   g. {1, 4, 6}
   h. {7, 8, 9}
   j. {4, 6, 8}
   k. NH

4. Which is the subset of the solution set for the inequality 4y < 12?

   f. {4, 5, 6}
   g. {3, 4, 5}
   h. {1, 2, 3}
   j. {0, 1, 2}
   k. NH

9. Which is the subset of the solution set for the inequality 8y > 64?

   a. {4, 6, 8}
   b. {2, 6, 10}
   c. {6, 7, 8}
   d. {9, 10, 12}
   e. NH

5. Which is the subset of the solution set for the inequality 7y > 21?

   a. {0, 1, 2}
   b. {4, 6, 8}
   c. {3, 5, 7}
   d. {2, 4, 6}
   e. NH

10. Which is the subset of the solution set for the inequality 9y < 72?

   f. {4, 6, 8}
   g. {2, 4, 6}
   h. {7, 9, 11}
   j. {6, 8, 10}
   k. NH

Directions

Read each question and choose the correct answer. Mark the space for the answer you have chosen. Mark NH if the answer is not here.

1. $2\frac{1}{3} + 8\frac{1}{2} =$

   a. $10\frac{2}{5}$ **d.** $10\frac{1}{6}$

   b. $10\frac{3}{5}$ **e.** NH

   c. $10\frac{5}{6}$

6. Estimate the answer by rounding:
$59.899 \div 11.879$

   f. 4
   g. 6
   h. 7
   j. 5
   k. NH

2. If $n = 9$, then $6n - 3 =$

   f. 12
   g. 51
   h. 53
   j. 57
   k. NH

7. If $n + 8 = 14$, then $n =$

   a. 9
   b. 8
   c. 7
   d. 6
   e. NH

3. $6 \times 884 =$

   a. 5,304
   b. 5,088
   c. 4,848
   d. 4,864
   e. NH

8. Which is the subset of the solution set for the inequality $9y > 45$?

   f. {3, 4, 5}
   g. {6, 8, 10}
   h. {5, 7, 9}
   j. {4, 6, 8}
   k. NH

4. $\frac{1}{3} \div \frac{1}{9} =$

   f. $\frac{1}{29}$ **j.** $\frac{1}{3}$

   g. $\frac{1}{9}$ **k.** NH

   h. 3

9. The quotient of $446.589 \div 8.114$ is between which numbers?

   a. 60 and 70
   b. 50 and 60
   c. 40 and 50
   d. 30 and 40
   e. NH

5. $\$5.72 + \$8.90 =$

   a. $13.52
   b. $14.62
   c. $14.72
   d. $14.79
   e. NH

10. $9.7 - 2.34 =$

   f. 1.37
   g. 7.44
   h. 7.34
   j. 7.36
   k. NH

Directions

Read each question and choose the correct answer. Mark the space for the answer you have chosen. Mark NH if the answer is not here.

---

1. $12,250 \div 14 =$

    a. 684
    b. 875
    c. 885
    d. 894
    e. NH

6. The quotient of $8,829 \div 90$ is between which numbers?

    f. 60 and 70
    g. 70 and 80
    h. 80 and 90
    j. 90 and 100
    k. NH

---

2. If $\frac{n}{3} = 7$, then $n =$

    f. 7
    g. 14
    h. 21
    j. 28
    k. NH

7. If $\frac{3}{12} = \frac{4}{y}$, then $y =$

    a. 16
    b. 8
    c. 12
    d. 14
    e. NH

---

3. 2 is 10% of what number?

    a. 200
    b. 0.2
    c. 2.0
    d. 20
    e. NH

8. Which is the subset of the solution set for the inequality $4y > 12$?

    f. {2, 4, 6}
    g. {5, 7, 9}
    h. {1, 3, 5}
    j. {3, 4, 5}
    k. NH

---

4. $\frac{4}{9} \times \frac{3}{6} =$

    f. $\frac{2}{9}$ j. $\frac{4}{9}$

    g. $\frac{3}{4}$ k. NH

    h. $\frac{7}{15}$

9. $8.7 \times 19 =$

    a. 1653
    b. 165.3
    c. 16.53
    d. 1.653
    e. NH

---

5. $5.2 \div 8 =$

    a. 65
    b. 6.5
    c. 0.65
    d. 0.065
    e. NH

10. $0.248 \times 3 =$

    f. 74.4
    g. 7.44
    h. 0.744
    j. 0.0744
    k. NH

Directions

Read each question and choose the correct answer. Mark the space for the answer you have chosen. Mark NH if the answer is not here.

1. $4\frac{1}{2} \div 4 =$

    a. $\frac{8}{9}$ d. 1

    b. $1\frac{1}{8}$ e. NH

    c. $\frac{7}{8}$

6. What is 3% of 500?

    f. 15
    g. 150
    h. 1,500
    j. 1.5
    k. NH

2. $17 - 8.234 =$

    f. 9.776
    g. 9.234
    h. 8.926
    j. 8.766
    k. NH

7. $56.72 + $18.94 =$

    a. $74.66
    b. $75.66
    c. $75.76
    d. $76.86
    e. NH

3. If $n - 8 = 5$, then $n =$

    a. 11
    b. 12
    c. 13
    d. 14
    e. NH

8. If $n = 12$, then $4n + 8 =$

    f. 48
    g. 52
    h. 54
    j. 56
    k. NH

4. If $n - 2 = 11$, then $n =$

    f. 13
    g. 12
    h. 10
    j. 9
    k. NH

9. $\frac{5}{8} - \frac{1}{4} =$

    a. $\frac{3}{8}$ d. 1

    b. $\frac{1}{4}$ e. NH

    c. $\frac{1}{8}$

5. $18.6 \div 0.02 =$

    a. 9,300
    b. 930
    c. 93
    d. 9.3
    e. NH

10. If $\frac{5}{6} = \frac{a}{18}$, then $a =$

    f. 8
    g. 15
    h. 25
    j. 20
    k. NH

Directions
Read each question and choose the correct answer. Mark the space for the answer you have chosen. Mark NH if the answer is not here.

---

1. $5\frac{1}{5} \times 2\frac{1}{2} =$

    a. $10\frac{1}{7}$ d. 12

    b. 13   e. NH

    c. $10\frac{2}{3}$

6. $0.5 \times 3.2 =$

    f. 160
    g. 16.0
    h. 1.6
    j. 0.16
    k. NH

---

2. If $\frac{3}{9} = \frac{b}{15}$, then b =

    f. 5
    g. 6
    h. 7
    j. 8
    k. NH

7. 5 is 20% of what number?

    a. 25
    b. 20
    c. 2.5
    d. 200
    e. NH

---

3. The quotient of $71.897 \div 9.023$ is closest to which number?

    a. 8
    b. 9
    c. 10
    d. 11
    e. NH

8. $52 \times 36 =$

    f. 1,512
    g. 1,827
    h. 1,872
    j. 1,982
    k. NH

---

4. If n = 9, then 3n + 5 =

    f. 17
    g. 27
    h. 32
    j. 35
    k. NH

9. If $\frac{n}{7} = 5$, then n =

    a. 12
    b. 15
    c. 25
    d. 35
    e. NH

---

5. $5,489 \div 60$ is between which numbers?

    a. 80 and 90
    b. 90 and 100
    c. 100 and 110
    d. 110 and 120
    e. NH

10. Which is the subset of the solution set for the inequality 5y > 25?

    f. {2, 3, 4}
    g. {6, 8, 10}
    h. {3, 5, 7}
    j. {3, 4, 5}
    k. NH

Directions
Read each question and choose the correct answer. Mark the space for the answer you have chosen. Mark NH if the answer is not here.

---

1. If $n - 3 = 8$, then $n =$

   a. 11
   b. 10
   c. 9
   d. 8
   e. NH

6. $3\frac{3}{4} - 1\frac{1}{6} =$

   f. $2\frac{1}{2}$ j. $2\frac{3}{4}$

   g. $2\frac{7}{12}$ k. NH

   h. $2\frac{2}{3}$

---

2. The quotient of $53.98 \div 5.996$ is closest to which number?

   f. 8
   g. 9
   h. 10
   j. 11
   k. NH

7. Which is the subset of the solution set for the inequality $3y > 27$?

   a. {10, 12, 14}
   b. {7, 8, 9}
   c. {4, 8, 12}
   d. {1, 2, 5}
   e. NH

---

3. $45.98 + 6.234 =$

   a. 5.224
   b. 10.832
   c. 108.32
   d. 52.214
   e. NH

8. If $6n = 48$, then $n =$

   f. 5
   g. 6
   h. 7
   j. 8
   k. NH

---

4. $\frac{2}{3} \times \frac{1}{2} =$

   f. $\frac{2}{5}$ j. $\frac{2}{3}$

   g. $\frac{3}{5}$ k. NH

   h. $\frac{1}{3}$

9. The quotient of $2857 \div 60$ is between which numbers?

   a. 20 and 30
   b. 30 and 40
   c. 40 and 50
   d. 50 and 60
   e. NH

---

5. 4% of 400 =

   a. 0.16
   b. 1.6
   c. 16
   d. 160
   e. NH

10. $7\frac{1}{2} \div 8 =$

   f. $1\frac{1}{16}$ j. $\frac{7}{16}$

   g. $\frac{15}{16}$ k. NH

   h. $56\frac{1}{2}$

Directions
Read each question and choose the correct answer. Mark the space for the answer you have chosen. Mark NH if the answer is not here.

---

1. If $n + 3 = 8$, then $n =$

   a. 2
   b. 3
   c. 4
   d. 5
   e. NH

6. $12.34 + $10 =

   f. $12.44
   g. $22.34
   h. $22.43
   j. $24.34
   k. NH

---

2. $4.59 \div 0.3 =$

   f. 0.153
   g. 1.53
   h. 15.3
   j. 153
   k. NH

7. $58 \times 91 =$

   a. 4,698
   b. 5,028
   c. 5,278
   d. 5,438
   e. NH

---

3. The quotient of $29.83 \div 7.4$ is closest to which number?

   a. 7
   b. 6
   c. 5
   d. 4
   e. NH

8. $\frac{1}{6} \div \frac{2}{3} =$

   f. $\frac{1}{4}$ j. $\frac{2}{16}$

   g. 4   k. NH

   h. $\frac{1}{9}$

---

4. 7 is what percent of 28?

   f. 10%
   g. 20%
   h. 25%
   j. 30%
   k. NH

9. $4\frac{5}{6} + 3\frac{1}{9} =$

   a. $7\frac{6}{15}$ d. $8\frac{1}{18}$

   b. $7\frac{2}{5}$ e. NH

   c. $7\frac{17}{18}$

---

5. $10 - 8.13 =$

   a. 2.13
   b. 1.87
   c. 1.83
   d. 1.13
   e. NH

10. 30% of 180 =

   f. 540
   g. 54
   h. 5.4
   j. 0.54
   k. NH

Directions

Read each question and choose the correct answer. Mark the space for the answer you have chosen. Mark NH if the answer is not here.

1. $4\frac{3}{4} \times 2\frac{1}{3} =$

  a. $8\frac{1}{4}$ d. 11

  b. 12   e. NH

  c. $11\frac{1}{12}$

6. $1.2 \times 5.4 =$

  f. 12
  g. 5.8
  h. 6.48
  j. 0.16
  k. NH

2. If $\frac{2}{3} = \frac{d}{18}$, then d =

  f. 5
  g. 6
  h. 7
  j. 8
  k. NH

7. 45% of 220 =

  a. 110
  b. 102
  c. 99
  d. 90
  e. NH

3. The quotient of 52.21 ÷ 8.03 is closest to ...

  a. 4
  b. 7
  c. 12
  d. 9
  e. NH

8. $86 \times 12 =$

  f. 1,488
  g. 1,032
  h. 2,031
  j. 1,548
  k. NH

4. If n = 4, then 8n x 2 =

  f. 16
  g. 32
  h. 24
  j. 34
  k. NH

9. If $\frac{n}{6} = 4$, then n =

  a. 24
  b. 18
  c. 9
  d. 36
  e. NH

5. 6,214 ÷ 20 is between which numbers?

  a. 350 and 370
  b. 115 and 135
  c. 250 and 270
  d. 300 and 320
  e. NH

10. $22.78 + $4.96 =

  f. $27.74
  g. $32.58
  h. $19.56
  j. $22.15
  k. NH

Directions

Read each question and choose the correct answer. Mark the space for the answer you have chosen. Mark NH if the answer is not here.

1. $3\frac{1}{2} \div 2 =$

  a. $\frac{4}{7}$ d. 5

  b. $1\frac{3}{4}$ e. NH

  c. $\frac{7}{8}$

2. $35 - 7.45 =$

  f. 12.52
  g. 26.89
  h. 27.55
  j. 10.63
  k. NH

3. If $n - 16 = 11$, then $n =$

  a. 41
  b. 35
  c. 27
  d. 13
  e. NH

4. If $25 - n = 14$, then $n =$

  f. 11
  g. 12
  h. 18
  j. 9
  k. NH

5. $9.3 \div 0.03 =$

  a. 310
  b. .310
  c. 3.10
  d. 31.0
  e. NH

6. What is 3% of 500?

  f. 15
  g. 150
  h. 1,500
  j. 1.5
  k. NH

7. $\$15.98 - \$13.47 =$

  a. $2.51
  b. $5.21
  c. $3.62
  d. $14.50
  e. NH

8. If $n = 8$, then $3n + 3 =$

  f. 30
  g. 29
  h. 28
  j. 27
  k. NH

9. $\frac{3}{8} - \frac{1}{4} =$

  a. $\frac{3}{8}$ d. 1

  b. $\frac{1}{4}$ e. NH

  c. $\frac{1}{8}$

10. If $\frac{2}{6} = \frac{c}{24}$, then $c =$

  f. 14
  g. 11
  h. 8
  j. 12
  k. NH

Name _____

Directions

Read each question and choose the correct answer. Mark the space for the answer you have chosen. Mark NH if the answer is not here.

1. One winter day the thermometer registered – 4°F. What would the thermometer read if the temperature went up 25°?

   a. 3° F
   b. 12° F
   c. 14° F
   d. 21° F
   e. NH

2. Johnny gained 8 yards on one running play, but lost 11 yards on the next. What was his total yard gain or loss for the two plays?

   f. 3 yd
   g. 19 yd
   h. – 3 yd
   j. – 19 yd
   k. NH

3. The actual temperature is 45°F. The wind chill makes it feel 12° colder. What temperature does it actually feel like today?

   a. 20° F
   b. 18° F
   c. 33° F
   d. 36° F
   e. NH

4. Mr. Lopez's balance in his savings account was $357.48. He withdrew $22.41. What is his new balance?

   f. $412.58
   g. $335.07
   h. $125.95
   j. $150.24
   k. NH

5. An elevator on the 18th floor goes down 16 floors. On which floor is the elevator now?

   a. 2nd
   b. 3rd
   c. 4th
   d. 5th
   e. NH

6. The jet was flying at an altitude of 20,000 feet. To avoid a storm, the pilot dropped it 5,540 feet. How high is the plane now?

   f. 32,514 ft
   g. 14,460 ft
   h. 12,855 ft
   j. 10,458 ft
   k. NH

7. The temperature at 6 PM was 20°F. By midnight it had fallen 12°. What was the temperature at midnight?

   a. 6° F
   b. 7° F
   c. 8° F
   d. 10° F
   e. NH

8. On two plays the Wildcats gained 4 yards and lost 9 yards. What was the team's net gain on the two plays?

   f. 13 yd
   g. – 13 yd
   h. – 5 yd
   j. 5 yd
   k. NH

9. The temperature seven hours ago was 5°F. Now the thermometer reads 22°F. How much did the temperature change?

   a. 27° F
   b. 22° F
   c. 17° F
   d. 15° F
   e. NH

10. The mountain's elevation is 3,426 ft. The valley is 1,245 feet below sea level. What is the difference in their elevation?

   f. 2,181 ft
   g. 4,671 ft
   h. 2,221 ft
   j. 4,661 ft
   k. NH

Directions

Read each question and choose the correct answer. Mark the space for the answer you have chosen. Mark NH if the answer is not here.

1. The Jets gained 5 yards, lost 8 yards, then lost 3 yards. What was their net gain for the three plays?

   a.   0 yd
   b.   − 3 yd
   c.   − 6 yd
   d. − 13 yd
   e.   NH

2. Mr. Banks had $235 in his account. He wrote a check for $10, another for $35, and deposited $20. What is his new balance?

   f. $300
   g. $280
   h. $240
   j. $210
   k.   NH

3. The boat was speeding along at 45 mph. It decreased its speed by 25 mph, then increased it by 10 mph. How fast is it going?

   a.   30 mph
   b.   40 mph
   c.   50 mph
   d.   70 mph
   e.   NH

4. At 10 a.m. the temperature was 8°C. By 2 p.m. it had dropped 6°. By 5 p.m. it dropped 7° more. What is the temperature at 5 p.m.?

   f.   7° C
   g.   −5° C
   h.   −7° C
   j.   9° C
   k.   NH

5. The airplane was flying at 4,000 m. It went up 500 m, then went down 1,000 m. At what altitude is the plane flying now?

   a.   2,500 m
   b.   5,500 m
   c.   3,500 m
   d.   5,000 m
   e.   NH

6. The elevator stopped on the 6th floor. It went up 8 floors and down 9 floors. At what floor is the elevator now?

   f.   4th
   g.   5th
   h.   6th
   j.   7th
   k.   NH

7. A stock opened the day selling for $12.50. During the day it rose $1.32 then fell $2.68. What is the selling price now?

   a. $1.32
   b. $13.86
   c. $12.52
   d. $11.14
   e.   NH

8. The temperature is 14°F. The wind chill is − 8°F. How much colder is the wind chill temperature than the actual temperature?

   f.   6° F
   g.   22° F
   h.   − 6° F
   j.   − 22° F
   k.   NH

9. The hikers started at 150 m. above sea level. They climbed to an elevation of 670 m. How many meters did they climb?

   a.   490 m
   b.   510 m
   c.   520 m
   d.   820 m
   e.   NH

10. Jasmine had $15.75 in her pocket when she found $1 on the ground. She spent $4.95 on lunch. How much does she have left?

    f. $11.80
    g. $10.80
    h. $10.50
    j. $9.80
    k.   NH

Directions

Use the coordinate points to answer the questions. Read each question and choose the correct answer. Mark the space for the answer you have chosen. Mark NH if the answer is not here.

Given the following:

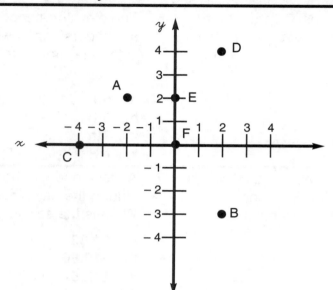

1. What are the coordinates of point A?

    a. (2, – 2)
    b. (– 2, – 2)
    c. (– 2, 2)
    d. (2, 2)
    e. NH

4. What are the coordinates of point D?

    f. (2, 4)
    g. (4, 2)
    h. (2, – 4)
    j. (– 4, 2)
    k. NH

2. What are the coordinates of point B?

    f. (– 1, 3)
    g. (2, – 3)
    h. (– 1, – 3)
    j. (– 3, 1)
    k. NH

5. What are the coordinates of point E?

    a. (2, 0)
    b. (0, 2)
    c. (– 2, 0)
    d. (0, – 2)
    e. NH

3. What are the coordinates of point C?

    a. (0, – 4)
    b. (4, 0)
    c. (– 4, – 4)
    d. (– 4, 0)
    e. NH

6. What are the coordinates of point F?

    f. (2, 2)
    g. (1, 1)
    h. (0, 0)
    j. (1, 0)
    k. NH

Directions
Read each question and choose the correct answer. Mark the space for the answer you have chosen. Mark NH if the answer is not here.

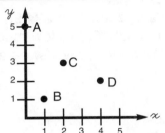

1. At which point does x = 3 and y = 2?

   a. **A**
   b. **B**
   c. **C**
   d. **D**
   e. **NH**

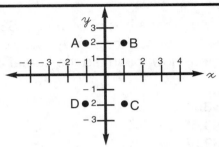

4. At which point does x = **1** and y = 2?

   f. **A**
   g. **B**
   h. **C**
   j. **D**
   k. **NH**

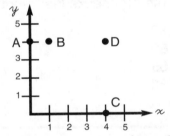

2. At which point does x = 4 and y = 0?

   f. **A**
   g. **B**
   h. **C**
   j. **D**
   k. **NH**

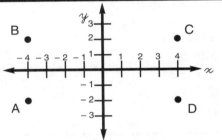

5. Which point is located at (4, –2)?

   a. **A**
   b. **B**
   c. **C**
   d. **D**
   e. **NH**

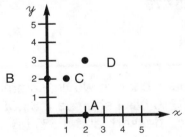

3. At which point does x = 0 and y = 2?

   a. **A**
   b. **B**
   c. **C**
   d. **D**
   e. **NH**

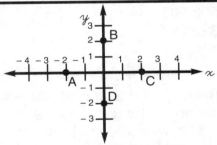

6. Which point is located at (0, –2)?

   f. **A**
   g. **B**
   h. **C**
   j. **D**
   k. **NH**

Directions

Read each question and choose the correct answer. Mark the space for the answer you have chosen. Mark NH if the answer is not here.

1. Lenny bought a box of cereal for $3.68 and he had a coupon for 35¢. A 3% tax was charged. How much did the cereal cost?

   a. $3.43
   b. $3.58
   c. $3.68
   d. $4.03
   e. NH

2. Jessica had $154.50 in her savings account. She bought a CD player for $129.99 plus 6% tax. How much money did she have left?

   f. $140.39
   g. $24.51
   h. $14.39
   j. $16.71
   k. NH

3. Tran's favorite cologne cost $25. If tax is 6%, how much change did she receive from $50?

   a. $26.75
   b. $25.00
   c. $23.50
   d. $22.25
   e. NH

4. On Tuesdays, burgers cost 39¢ each. Big Joe ordered 5 burgers and a 99¢ order of fries. If tax was 6%, what was his total bill?

   f. $1.49
   g. $2.96
   h. $3.24
   j. $3.66
   k. NH

5. Monica's sweater cost $24.95 and Lacey's sweater cost $16.99. How much less expensive was Lacey's sweater?

   a. $8.06
   b. $8.04
   c. $7.98
   d. $7.96
   e. NH

6. The bank charges $2.50 each month for a checking account and 15¢ for each check written. How much would it cost a customer who wrote 12 checks last month?

   f. $1.80
   g. $2.50
   h. $2.65
   j. $4.30
   k. NH

7. J'Ani earns $5.95 per hour. She works 15 hours each week. How much will she earn in four weeks?

   a. $89.25
   b. $178.50
   c. $267.75
   d. $357
   e. NH

8. How much change would Kammi receive from a $10 bill if she spent $5.68 on lunch, $1.59 on dessert, and a 5% tax was added?

   f. $2.37
   g. $3.32
   h. $4.32
   j. $4.93
   k. NH

Name _____

Directions
Read each question and choose the correct answer. Mark the space for the answer you have chosen. Mark NH if the answer is not here.

1. Tasha bought raspberry lotion for each of her three friends. If each lotion cost $3.49, how much did she spend, including 5% sales tax?

   a. $3.49
   b. $9.49
   c. $9.97
   d. $10.99
   e. NH

2. Darrel bought tickets to the water park for himself and his three children. If adult tickets cost $16.95 and children's tickets cost $11.95, how much did he spend in all?

   f. $28.90
   g. $35.85
   h. $52.80
   j. $62.80
   k. NH

3. Lin receives $3.50 a week for allowance. How many weeks must he save his allowance to buy a CD which costs $11.99?

   a. 2 weeks
   b. 3 weeks
   c. 4 weeks
   d. 5 weeks
   e. NH

4. James spent $3.37 for breakfast, $5.76 for lunch, and $14.52 for dinner. He also had two snacks which cost $1.75 each. How much did James spend on food that day?

   f. $27.15
   g. $25.40
   h. $25.25
   j. $23.65
   k. NH

5. The 11 girls on the all-star basketball team held a bake sale to raise money. If they each earned $50, how much did they raise in all?

   a. $55
   b. $500
   c. $550
   d. $600
   e. NH

6. Juan spent $4.35 on his lunch. Tax was 4%. How much change did Juan receive if he paid with a $5 bill?

   f. $0.65
   g. $0.48
   h. $0.45
   j. $0.38
   k. NH

7. A ticket to the concert cost $21.95. A 75¢ handling charge is added to the price of each ticket. How much would 4 tickets and their handling charges cost?

   a. $22.70
   b. $87.80
   c. $88.55
   d. $90.80
   e. NH

8. A sweater costs $16.99. A sweatshirt is on sale for $23.95. How much less expensive is the sweater than the sweatshirt?

   f. $5.69
   g. $5.96
   h. $6.04
   j. $6.50
   k. NH

Directions
Read each question and choose the correct answer. Mark the space for the answer you have chosen. Mark NH if the answer is not here.

1. Amanda grew 3 inches in six months. What was her average growth per month?

   a.   0.5 in
   b.   0.75 in
   c.   1.5 in
   d.   2 in
   e.   NH

2. Jayme scored 12, 15, 11, and 8 points in her last four basketball games. What was the average number of points she scored for each game?

   f.   10.5
   g.   11
   h.   11.5
   j.   12
   k.   NH

3. Hillsville received five inches of snow on Monday, 7.5 on Tuesday, 3 on Wednesday, 0.5 on Thursday, and 6 inches on Friday. What was the average snowfall for each day?

   a.   4 in
   b.   4.4 in
   c.   4.8 in
   d.   5.5 in
   e.   NH

4. The middle school football team's offensive linemen weigh 201 lb, 152 lb, 168 lb, and 190 lb. What is their average weight?

   f.   175 lb
   g.   177.75 lb
   h.   178.25 lb
   j.   180.5 lb
   k.   NH

5. A light bulb should last for 1,500 hours. If the bulb is used for an average of 10 hours per day, how many days should the bulb last?

   a.   150 days
   b.   155 days
   c.   1,500 days
   d.   15,000 days
   e.   NH

6. Salaam earned $251.62 one week and $185.14 the next. What was his average earnings?

   f. $436.76
   g. $260.48
   h. $218.38
   j. $145.59
   k.   NH

7. Justin earned scores of 73, 94, and 85 on three tests in algebra. What is his average score on the tests?

   a.   80
   b.   82
   c.   84
   d.   86
   e.   NH

8. The temperature was 8° above normal yesterday and 6° above normal today. What is the average of these two temperatures?

   f.   6° above normal
   g.   7° above normal
   h.   8° above normal
   j.   14° above normal
   k.   NH

Directions
Read each question and choose the correct answer. Mark the space for the answer you have chosen. Mark NH if the answer is not here.

1. Jackie studied five hours on Monday, three hours on Tuesday, and four hours on Wednesday. What is the average number of hours she studied each day?

    a. 2
    b. 3
    c. 4
    d. 5
    e. NH

2. Julie received the following math grades last week: 92, 88, 85, 96, and 89. What is the average math grade Julie received last week?

    f. 88
    g. 89
    h. 90
    j. 9
    k. NH

3. Henry played five rounds of golf and received the following scores: 87, 88, 92, 78, 90. What is Henry's average golf score for each game?

    a. 88
    b. 87
    c. 89
    d. 90
    e. NH

4. Ruth has five friends in Ohio, six friends in New York, four friends in Texas, and nine friends in Kansas. What is the average number of friends Ruth has in each state?

    f. 5
    g. 6
    h. 7
    j. 8
    k. NH

5. Jim mows lawns for extra money. He mowed 9 lawns one week, 12 the next week, and 15 the week after that. How many lawns did he mow on average each week?

    a. 9
    b. 12
    c. 15
    d. 18
    e. NH

6. Peggy bought three dresses. One cost $52.50, one cost $48.25, and the other cost $51.95. What is the average cost of each dress that Peggy bought?

    f. $50.82
    g. $49.81
    h. $51.23
    j. $50.90
    k. NH

7. Paula saw 12 red cars on the way to school today and 18 red cars yesterday. What is the average number of red cars she saw today and yesterday?

    a. 13
    b. 15
    c. 17
    d. 19
    e. NH

8. John ran eight miles yesterday and six miles today, and he will run 10 miles tomorrow. What is the average number of miles he will have run each day?

    f. 6
    g. 7
    h. 8
    j. 10
    k. NH

Name _____

Directions
Read each question and choose the correct answer. Mark the space for the answer you have chosen. Mark NH if the answer is not here.

1. When making marshmallow treats, we add 1 cup of marshmallows to every 6 cups of cereal. How many cups of marshmallows would you need for 15 cups of cereal?

   a. 4 cups
   b. 3.5 cups
   c. 2.5 cups
   d. 2 cups
   e. NH

2. If it takes 3 hours to bake a 10-pound turkey, how many hours will it take to bake a 15-pound turkey?

   f. 3.75 hours
   g. 4 hours
   h. 4.5 hours
   j. 5 hours
   k. NH

3. When painting, we use six cans of yellow paint to every two cans of red paint. How much red paint is needed if we have 12 cans of yellow paint?

   a. 4 cans
   b. 6 cans
   c. 14 cans
   d. 36 cans
   e. NH

4. During our week at camp we spent 3 hours hiking for every one hour we rested. How long did we rest if we hiked for 12 hours?

   f. 3 hours
   g. 4 hours
   h. 6 hours
   j. 36 hours
   k. NH

5. In our class, there are 3 boys for every 2 girls. How many girls are in the class if there are 18 boys?

   a. 10
   b. 12
   c. 14
   d. 16
   e. NH

6. Sandy solved 5 word problems in 25 minutes. At this rate, how many minutes will it take her to solve nine problems?

   f. 35 minutes
   g. 40 minutes
   h. 45 minutes
   j. 50 minutes
   k. NH

7. On the map, you must move 2 inches north for every 5 inches west. If you move 10 inches west, how many inches should you move north?

   a. 25 in
   b. 20 in
   c. 8 in
   d. 4 in
   e. NH

8. The science experiment calls for 4 ml of solution A for every 5 ml of solution B. If we use 20 ml of solution B, how many ml of solution A should we use?

   f. 8 ml
   g. 10 ml
   h. 16 ml
   j. 25 ml
   k. NH

Directions
Read each question and choose the correct answer. Mark the space for the answer you have chosen. Mark NH if the answer is not here.

---

1. A bag contains 6 red balls, 7 green balls, and 4 yellow balls. What is the probability that a ball you choose at random will be yellow?

   a. $\frac{13}{17}$ d. $\frac{4}{13}$

   b. $\frac{4}{17}$ e. NH

   c. $\frac{7}{17}$

5. If you roll a six-sided die, what is the probability that you will roll a 4 or a 5?

   a. $\frac{1}{6}$ d. $\frac{4}{6}$

   b. $\frac{2}{6}$ e. NH

   c. $\frac{3}{6}$

---

2. A bag contains 6 red balls, 7 green balls, and 4 yellow balls. What is the probability that a ball you choose at random will be red or yellow?

   f. $\frac{10}{17}$ j. $\frac{13}{17}$

   g. $\frac{4}{17}$ k. NH

   h. $\frac{11}{17}$

6. If you choose a day of the week at random, what is the probability that it will have a "d" in its name?

   f. $\frac{0}{7}$ j. $\frac{2}{7}$

   g. $\frac{1}{7}$ k. NH

   h. $\frac{7}{7}$

---

3. A bag contains 6 red balls, 7 green balls, and 4 yellow balls. What is the probability that a ball you choose at random will <u>not</u> be red?

   a. $\frac{6}{17}$ d. $\frac{13}{17}$

   b. $\frac{10}{17}$ e. NH

   c. $\frac{11}{17}$

7. If you pick a month of the year at random, what is the probability that its name will start with the letter "J"?

   a. $\frac{2}{12}$ d. $\frac{3}{12}$

   b. $\frac{1}{12}$ e. NH

   c. $\frac{7}{12}$

---

4. If you roll a six-sided die, what is the probability that you will roll a 1?

   f. $\frac{1}{5}$ j. $\frac{5}{6}$

   g. $\frac{1}{6}$ k. NH

   h. $\frac{2}{6}$

8. If you roll a six-sided die, what is the probability that you will roll a seven?

   f. $\frac{1}{6}$ j. $\frac{2}{6}$

   g. $\frac{0}{6}$ k. NH

   h. $\frac{7}{6}$

Name _____

Directions

Read each question and choose the number sentence you can use to find each answer. Mark the space for the number sentence you have chosen. Mark NH if the answer is not here.

---

1. Amy bought two packs of index cards for 40¢ each. If there is no tax, how much change will she receive from $1.00?

    a. $2 \times .40 - 1 = n$
    b. $1 - (2 \times .40) = n$
    c. $1 - (2 \div .40) = n$
    d. $1 + (2 \times .40) = n$
    e. NH

5. Lupe bought 4 peppermints at 2¢ each. How much change did she receive from a dime? (There was no tax.)

    a. $.10 - (4 \times .02) = n$
    b. $(.02 \times .10) - 4 = n$
    c. $(.10 - .02) \div 4 = n$
    d. $.10 - (4 \div .02) = n$
    e. NH

---

2. Franco bought three candy canes for 7¢ each. If there is no tax, how much change will he receive from a quarter?

    f. $.25 + (3 \div .07) = n$
    g. $3 \times .07 - .25 = n$
    h. $.25 - (3 \times .07) = n$
    j. $(.25 - .07) \div 3 = n$
    k. NH

6. Rocky bought 6 pieces of chalk at 3¢ each. How much change did he receive from a quarter? (There was no tax.)

    f. $.25 - (6 - .03) = n$
    g. $.25 - (6 \div .03) = n$
    h. $.25 - (6 \times .03) = n$
    j. $.25 - (6 + .03) = n$
    k. NH

---

3. Abram bought three licorice sticks for 6¢ each. If there is no tax, how much change will he receive from a half dollar?

    a. $.50 - (3 \times .06) = n$
    b. $(.50 - 3) \times .06 = n$
    c. $.06 (.50 \div 3) = n$
    d. $.50 + (3 \times .06) = n$
    e. NH

7. Will purchased four pencils at 4¢ each. How much change did he receive from a quarter? (There was no tax.)

    a. $.25 - (4 \div .04) = n$
    b. $.25 - (4 - .04) = n$
    c. $.25 - (4 \times .04) = n$
    d. $.25 - (4 + .04) = n$
    e. NH

---

4. Jordan purchased four candy bars for 60¢ each. How much change will he receive from a $5 bill if there is no tax?

    f. $5.00 - .60 \div 4 = n$
    g. $.60 - (5.00 \div 4) = n$
    h. $(5.00 \div .60) \times 4 = n$
    j. $5.00 - (4 \times .60) = n$
    k. NH

8. Keion bought two 33¢ postage stamps. How much change did she receive from $1.00? (There was no tax.)

    f. $1.00 - (2 \times .33) = n$
    g. $1.00 \div (.33 \div 2) = n$
    h. $1.00 \times (.33 + 2) = n$
    j. $1.00 - (.33 \div 2) = n$
    k. NH

Directions

Read each question and choose the correct answer. Mark the space for the answer you have chosen. Mark NH if the answer is not here.

1. Which number sentence means,
   "the difference of a number and 3 is 14"?

   a. $3 - n = 14$
   b. $n + 3 = 14$
   c. $3n = 14$
   d. $n - 3 = 14$
   e. NH

5. Which equation means,
   "the quotient of 7 times a number and 3 is 12"?

   a. $7n + 3 = 12$
   b. $7(n \div 3) = 12$
   c. $7n - 3 = 12$
   d. $7n \div 3 = 12$
   e. NH

2. Which equation means,
   "the sum of twice a number and 2 is -5"?

   f. $2(n + 2) = -5$
   g. $2n - 2 = 5$
   h. $2n + 2 = -5$
   j. $2n - 2 = -5$
   k. NH

6. Which number sentence means,
   "four times the sum of a number and 3 is 6"?

   f. $4(n + 3) = 6$
   g. $4n + 3 = 6$
   h. $4n - 3 = 6$
   j. $4n \div 3 = 6$
   k. NH

3. Which equation means,
   "the product of a number and 7 is 21"?

   a. $7 + n = 21$
   b. $7n = 21$
   c. $n - 7 = 21$
   d. $n \div 7 = 21$
   e. NH

7. Which equation means,
   "seven more than 5 times a number is 18"?

   a. $5n - 7 = 18$
   b. $5n + 7 = 18$
   c. $5(n + 7) = 18$
   d. $5n + 18 = 7$
   e. NH

4. Which number sentence means,
   "three times the difference of a number and 1 is 8"?

   f. $3n - 1 = 8$
   g. $3n + 1 = 8$
   h. $3(n - 1) = 8$
   j. $3(n + 1) = 8$
   k. NH

8. Which equation means,
   "the quotient of a number and -2 is 11"?

   f. $n \div (-2) = 11$
   g. $-2n = 11$
   h. $-2 + n = 11$
   j. $n - (-2) = 11$
   k. NH

Name _____   Skill: Geometry (Lines, Line Segments, Rays)

Directions

Read each question and choose the correct answer. Mark the space for the answer you have chosen. Mark NH if the answer is not here.

---

1. Which of the following is a line?

a. 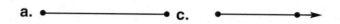   c.

b.   d.

e. NH

---

2. Which of the following is a line segment?

f.   h.

g.   j.

k. NH

---

3. Which of the following is a ray?

a.   c.

b.   d.

e. NH

---

4. What is the name of the following?

A   B

f.   Line AB
g.   Ray AB
h.   Line Segment AB
j.   Angle AB
k.   NH

---

5. What is the name of the following?

A   B

a.   Line AB
b.   Ray AB
c.   Line Segment AB
d.   Angle AB
e.   NH

---

6. What is the name of the following?

A   B

f.   Line AB
g.   Ray AB
h.   Line Segment AB
j.   Angle AB
k.   NH

---

7. Which of the following figures illustrates Line CD?

a.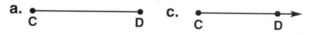
  C   D

c.
  C   D

b.
  C   D

d.
  C   R

e. NH

---

8. Which of the following figures illustrates Ray RS?

f.
  S   R

h.
  R   S

g.
  S   R

j.
  T   R

k. NH

Name _____   Skill: Geometry (Parallel, Intersecting, Perpendicular Lines)

Directions
Read each question and choose the correct answer. Mark the space for the answer you have chosen. Mark NH if the answer is not here.

1. Which word most accurately describes the following lines?

   a. Parallel
   b. Intersecting
   c. Perpendicular
   d. Acute
   e. NH

5. Which word most accurately describes the following lines?

   a. Parallel
   b. Intersecting
   c. Perpendicular
   d. Acute
   e. NH

2. Which word most accurately describes the following lines?

   f. Parallel
   g. Intersecting
   h. Perpendicular
   j. Acute
   k. NH

6. Which word most accurately describes the following lines?

   f. Parallel
   g. Intersecting
   h. Perpendicular
   j. Acute
   k. NH

3. Which word most accurately describes the following lines?

   a. Parallel
   b. Intersecting
   c. Perpendicular
   d. Acute
   e. NH

7. Which word most accurately describes the following lines?

   a. Parallel
   b. Intersecting
   c. Perpendicular
   d. Acute
   e. NH

4. Which word most accurately describes the following lines?

   f. Parallel
   g. Intersecting
   h. Perpendicular
   j. Acute
   k. NH

8. Which word most accurately describes the following lines?

   f. Parallel
   g. Intersecting
   h. Perpendicular
   j. Acute
   k. NH

Name _____

Directions

Read each question and choose the correct answer. Mark the space for the answer you have chosen. Mark NH if the answer is not here.

---

1. Which angle measures 45°?

a.

c.

b.

d.

e. NH

---

5. Which angle is <u>not</u> acute?

a.

c.

b.

d.

e. NH

---

2. Which angle is obtuse?

f.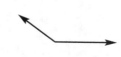

h.

g.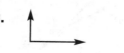

j.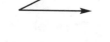

k. NH

---

6. Which angle measures about 70°?

f.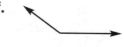

h.

g.

j.

k. NH

---

3. Which angle measures 90°?

a.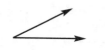

c.

b.

d.

e. NH

---

7. Which of the following could not be the measurement of an acute angle?

a. 90°
b. 87°
c. 40°
d. 2.5°
e. NH

---

4. Which angle measures about 120°?

f.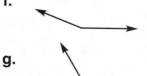

h.

g.

j.

k. NH

---

8. What is the measure of an acute angle?

f. exactly 180°
g. less than 180°
h. between 90° and 180°
j. less than 90°
k. NH

Directions
Read each question and choose the correct answer. Mark the space for the answer you have chosen. Mark NH if the answer is not here.

---

1. Name the figure shown below.

a. Line AB
b. Circle A
c. Ray AB
d. Ray A
e. NH

5. Name the figure shown below.

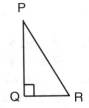

a. Right Triangle PQR
b. Acute Triangle PQR
c. Obtuse Triangle PQR
d. Oblong Triangle PQR
e. NH

---

2. Name the figure shown below.

f. Acute Angle
g. Right Angle
h. Obtuse Angle
j. Parallel Angle
k. NH

6. Name the figure shown below.

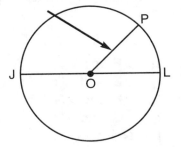

f. Chord OP
g. Ray OP
h. Radius P
j. Radius OP
k. NH

---

3. Name the figure shown below.

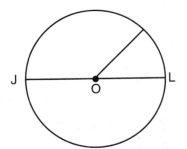

a. Circle O
b. Circle L
c. Circle JOL
d. Circle J
e. NH

7. Name the figure shown below.

a. Line AB
b. Line Segment AB
c. Line Fragment AB
d. Line Segment ABA
e. NH

---

4. Name the figure shown below.

f. Line A
g. Line Segment AB
h. Line AB
j. Double Ray AB
k. NH

8. Name the figure shown below.

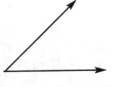

f. Acute Angle
g. Right Angle
h. Obtuse Angle
j. Parallel Angle
k. NH

Directions

Read each question and choose the correct answer. Mark the space for the answer you have chosen. Mark NH if the answer is not here.

1. Figures EFG and PQR are congruent. Which is a pair of corresponding points?

   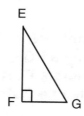

   a. **E and R**
   b. **P and F**
   c. **F and Q**
   d. **G and Q**
   e. **NH**

5. Figures JKLM and NOPQ are congruent. Which is a pair of corresponding sides?

   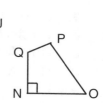

   a. $\overline{JK}$ and $\overline{NO}$
   b. $\overline{KL}$ and $\overline{ON}$
   c. $\overline{ML}$ and $\overline{NQ}$
   d. $\overline{KL}$ and $\overline{NQ}$
   e. **NH**

2. Figures EFG and PQR are congruent. Which is a pair of corresponding angles?

   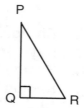

   f. **∠F and ∠Q**
   g. **∠E and ∠R**
   h. **∠E and ∠Q**
   j. **∠G and ∠P**
   k. **NH**

6. Figures ABCD and WXYZ are congruent. Which is a pair of corresponding points?

   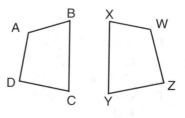

   f. **A and D**
   g. **B and Y**
   h. **C and X**
   j. **D and Z**
   k. **NH**

3. Figures EFG and PQR are congruent. Which is a pair of corresponding sides?

   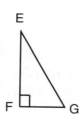
   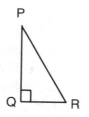

   a. $\overline{EG}$ and $\overline{PQ}$
   b. $\overline{FG}$ and $\overline{PR}$
   c. $\overline{FG}$ and $\overline{QR}$
   d. $\overline{EF}$ and $\overline{RQ}$
   e. **NH**

7. Figures ABCD and WXYZ are congruent. Which is a pair of corresponding angles?

   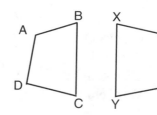

   a. **∠A and ∠Z**
   b. **∠B and ∠X**
   c. **∠C and ∠X**
   d. **∠D and ∠W**
   e. **NH**

4. Figures PQRS and VWXY are congruent. Which is a pair of corresponding sides?

   f. $\overline{PQ}$ and $\overline{WX}$
   g. $\overline{QR}$ and $\overline{VY}$
   h. $\overline{PS}$ and $\overline{VY}$
   j. $\overline{SR}$ and $\overline{WV}$
   k. **NH**

8. Figures ABCD and WXYZ are congruent. Which is a pair of corresponding sides?

   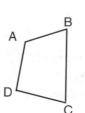
   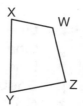

   f. $\overline{AB}$ and $\overline{WZ}$
   g. $\overline{AB}$ and $\overline{YZ}$
   h. $\overline{CD}$ and $\overline{XY}$
   j. $\overline{BC}$ and $\overline{XY}$
   k. **NH**

Directions
Read each question and choose the correct answer. Mark the space for the answer you have chosen. Mark NH if the answer is not here.

1. What is the measure of angle BCA given:

Angle ABC = 90°
Angle BAC = 50°

a. 70°
b. 60°
c. 50°
d. 40°
e. NH

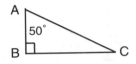

5. What is the measure of angle RST given:

Angle STR = 90°
Angle TRS = 50°

a. 60°
b. 50°
c. 40°
d. 30°
e. NH

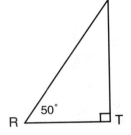

2. What is the measure of angle JLK given:

Angle LJK = 100°
Angle JKL = 50°

f. 30°
g. 40°
h. 50°
j. 60°
k. NH

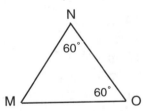

6. What is the measure of angle PRQ given:

Angle RPQ = 101°
Angle PQR = 39°

f. 20°
g. 30°
h. 40°
j. 50°
k. NH

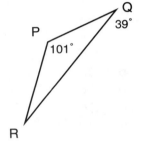

3. What is the measure of angle NMO given:

Angle NOM = 60°
Angle MNO = 60°

a. 40°
b. 50°
c. 60°
d. 70°
e. NH

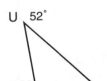

7. What is the measure of angle UVW given:

Angle VUW = 52°
Angle VWU = 25°

a. 113°
b. 103°
c. 93°
d. 83°
e. NH

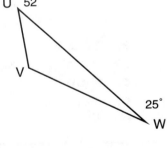

4. What is the measure of angle YZX given:

Angle XYZ = 80°
Angle YXZ = 40°

f. 50°
g. 60°
h. 70°
j. 80°
k. NH

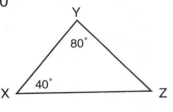

8. What is the measure of angle MTA given:

Angle MAT = 45°
Angle AMT = 65°

f. 50°
g. 60°
h. 70°
j. 80°
k. NH

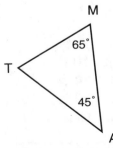

Directions

Read each question and choose the correct answer. Mark the space for the answer you have chosen. Mark NH if the answer is not here.

1. Which of the following is a radius of the circle?

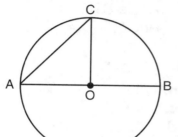

a. $\overline{AO}$
b. $\overline{AB}$
c. $\overline{AC}$
d. $\overarc{AC}$
e. NH

5. Which of the following is <u>not</u> a radius of the circle?

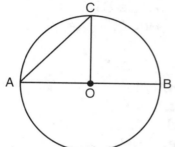

a. $\overline{OB}$
b. $\overline{AB}$
c. $\overline{OC}$
d. $\overline{OA}$
e. NH

2. Which of the following is a diameter of the circle?

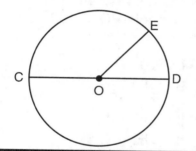

f. $\overline{CO}$
g. $\overline{OE}$
h. $\overline{OD}$
j. $\overline{CD}$
k. NH

6. Which of the following is a chord of the circle?

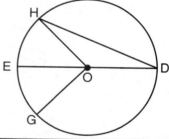

f. $\overline{OG}$
g. $\overline{GD}$
h. $\overline{EO}$
j. $\overline{FD}$
k. NH

3. If the measure of radius $\overline{OD}$ is 6 cm, what is the measure of $\overline{OF}$?

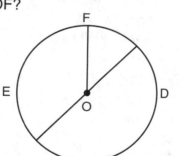

a. 12 cm
b. 8 cm
c. 6 cm
d. 3 cm
e. NH

7. The measure of radius $\overline{PO}$ is 8 m. What is the measure of $\overline{QR}$?

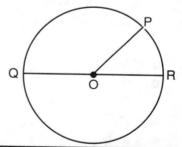

a. 14 m
b. 8 m
c. 16 m
d. 32 m
e. NH

4. The measure of diameter $\overline{LM}$ is 14 feet. What is the measure of $\overline{ON}$?

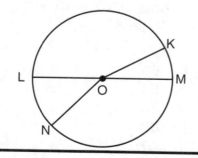

f. 7 ft
g. 10 ft
h. 14 ft
j. 28 ft
k. NH

8. Which of the following names an arc of the circle?

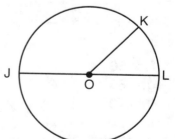

f. $\overline{JO}$
g. $\overline{JL}$
h. $\overarc{JL}$
j. $\overline{KO}$
k. NH

Directions
Read each question and choose the correct answer. Mark the space for the answer you have chosen. Mark NH if the answer is not here.

---

1. What is the perimeter of this triangle?

a. 63 m
b. 21.5 m
c. 20 m
d. 27 m
e. NH

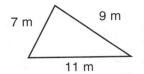

5. What is the perimeter of this triangle?

a. 30 mm
b. 40 mm
c. 50 mm
d. 60 mm
e. NH

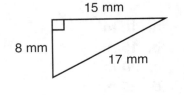

---

2. What is the perimeter of this parallelogram?

f. 16 in
g. 18 in
h. 20 in
j. 24 in
k. NH

6. What is the perimeter of this regular hexagon?

f. 24 cm
g. 20 cm
h. 48 cm
j. 32 cm
k. NH

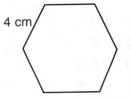

---

3. What is the perimeter of this square?

a. 24 cm
b. 36 cm
c. 12 cm
d. 6 cm
e. NH

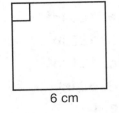

7. What is the perimeter of this parallelogram?

a. 32 cm
b. 164 cm
c. 288 cm
d. 66 cm
e. NH

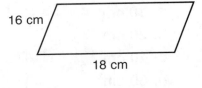

---

4. What is the perimeter of this rectangle?

f. 11 ft
g. 22 ft
h. 18 ft
j. 12 ft
k. NH

8. What is the perimeter of this trapezoid?

f. 14 m
g. 21 m
h. 28 m
j. 32 m
k. NH

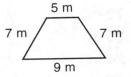

Directions

Read each question and choose the correct answer. Mark the space for the answer you have chosen. Mark NH if the answer is not here.

1. What is the area of this square in square meters?

   a. **10 m²**
   b. **15 m²**
   c. **20 m²**
   d. **25 m²**
   e. **NH**

   5m

2. What is the area of the triangle in square feet?

   f. **6 ft²**
   g. **12 ft²**
   h. **18 ft²**
   j. **24 ft²**
   k. **NH**

   4 ft
   6 ft

3. What is the area of this rectangle in square centimeters?

   a. **10 cm²**
   b. **20 cm²**
   c. **40 cm²**
   d. **80 cm²**
   e. **NH**

   5 cm
   8 cm

4. What is the area of this parallelogram in square inches?

   f. **72 in²**
   g. **36 in²**
   h. **24 in²**
   j. **20 in²**
   k. **NH**

   6 in
   12 in

5. A rectangular board is 4 feet wide and 10 feet long. What is the area of the board in square feet?

   a. **40 ft²**
   b. **36 ft²**
   c. **28 ft²**
   d. **20 ft²**
   e. **NH**

6. A rectangular card is 3 inches wide and 6 inches long. What is the area of the card in square inches?

   f. **4.5 in²**
   g. **9 in²**
   h. **18 in²**
   j. **28 in²**
   k. **NH**

7. A parallelogram has a base of 12 inches and a height of 11 inches. What is the area of the parallelogram in square inches?

   a. **144 in²**
   b. **132 in²**
   c. **121 in²**
   d. **66 in²**
   e. **NH**

8. What is the area of this polygon in square centimeters?

   f. **28 cm²**
   g. **58 cm²**
   h. **72 cm²**
   j. **144 cm²**
   k. **NH**

   7 cm
   6 cm
   4 cm
   12 cm

Directions

Read each question and choose the correct answer. Mark the space for the answer you have chosen. Mark NH if the answer is not here.

---

1. What is the volume of this box in cubic meters?

   a. 10 m³
   b. 20 m³
   c. 40 m³
   d. 80 m³
   e. NH

   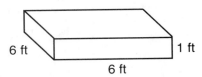

   7 m   8 m   5 m

---

5. What is the volume of this prism in cubic feet?

   a. 144 ft³
   b. 132 ft³
   c. 121 ft³
   d. 66 ft³
   e. NH

   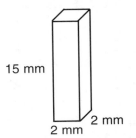

   6 ft   1 ft   6 ft

---

2. What is the volume of this cube in cubic inches?

   f. 15 in³
   g. 125 in³
   h. 25 in³
   j. 75 in³
   k. NH

   5 in   5 in   5 in

---

6. What is the volume of this prism in cubic millimeters?

   f. 120 mm³
   g. 60 mm³
   h. 40 mm³
   j. 19 mm³
   k. NH

   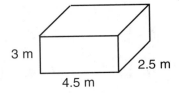

   15 mm   2 mm   2 mm

---

3. What is the volume of this figure in cubic feet?

   a. 150 ft³
   b. 54 ft³
   c. 120 ft³
   d. 226 ft³
   e. NH

   4 ft   5 ft   6 ft

---

7. What is the volume of this box in cubic meters?

   a. 42.75 m³
   b. 33.75 m³
   c. 22.75 m³
   d. 10 m³
   e. NH

   3 m   2.5 m   4.5 m

---

4. What is the volume of this box in cubic inches?

   f. 144 in³
   g. 140 in³
   h. 40 in³
   j. 19 in³
   k. NH

   3 in   4 in   12 in

---

8. What is the volume of this cube in cubic centimeters?

   f. 10 cm³
   g. 100 cm³
   h. 1,000 cm³
   j. 10,000 cm³
   k. NH

   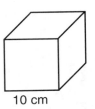

   10 cm

Name _____   Skill: Fraction Word Problems

Directions

Read each question and choose the correct answer. Mark the space for the answer you have chosen. Mark NH if the answer is not here.

---

1. Jamie wants to buy a CD player for $80. If he has saved $40, what fraction of the cost of the CD player does he have?

   a. $\frac{1}{8}$ d. $\frac{1}{2}$

   b. $\frac{1}{4}$ e. NH

   c. $\frac{1}{3}$

5. Lin has $30 saved toward the $90 bike she wants. What fraction of the cost of the bike does she now have?

   a. $\frac{3}{10}$ d. $\frac{1}{3}$

   b. $\frac{2}{3}$ e. NH

   c. $\frac{1}{2}$

---

2. Barbara has $35 set aside for a dress she likes. If the dress costs $105, what fraction of the cost has she saved?

   f. $\frac{1}{2}$ j. $\frac{1}{5}$

   g. $\frac{1}{3}$ k. NH

   h. $\frac{1}{4}$

6. Ternae is saving to buy a nice gift for her parents' anniversary. She has saved $15 and the gift she likes cost $30. What fraction of the cost has she saved?

   f. $\frac{1}{3}$ j. $\frac{1}{8}$

   g. $\frac{1}{2}$ k. NH

   h. $\frac{1}{4}$

---

3. Peggy wants to buy a sweater for $28. She has $7. What fraction of the price of the sweater does she have now?

   a. $\frac{1}{5}$ d. $\frac{1}{2}$

   b. $\frac{1}{4}$ e. NH

   c. $\frac{1}{3}$

7. Lenny has saved $45 towards the $60 skates he wants. What fraction of the selling price of the skates has he saved?

   a. $\frac{1}{5}$ d. $\frac{1}{2}$

   b. $\frac{2}{3}$ e. NH

   c. $\frac{3}{4}$

---

4. J.C. wants to buy a new video game that costs $60. He has saved $50 so far. What fraction of the selling price has he saved?

   f. $\frac{5}{6}$ j. $\frac{1}{4}$

   g. $\frac{1}{6}$ k. NH

   h. $\frac{2}{3}$

8. Brad wants a new aluminum baseball bat that costs $90. He earns $15 a week. He has saved 4 weeks of earnings. What fraction of the price of the bat has he saved?

   f. $\frac{1}{6}$ j. $\frac{2}{3}$

   g. $\frac{1}{3}$ k. NH

   h. $\frac{1}{2}$

Name _____

Directions
Read each question and choose the correct answer. Mark the space for the answer you have chosen. Mark NH if the answer is not here.

1. If Johnny paid 80¢ for a half pound of grapes, what was the cost per pound?

   a. 40¢
   b. 80¢
   c. $1.20
   d. $1.60
   e. NH

5. Lois bought $1/2$ of a pound of ham for $1.86. What was the cost per pound?

   a. 93¢
   b. $1.25
   c. $1.86
   d. $3.72
   e. NH

2. Penny paid 60¢ for $1/3$ of a pound of jelly beans. What does one full pound of jelly beans cost?

   f. 60¢
   g. $1.20
   h. $1.80
   j. $2.40
   k. NH

6. Tim purchased $1/3$ of a pound of raisins for 40¢. What is the cost for a pound of raisins?

   f. 20¢
   g. 40¢
   h. 80¢
   j. $1.20
   k. NH

3. Justin paid 50¢ for $1/4$ of a pound of candy. What was the cost per pound?

   a. $2.00
   b. $1.50
   c. 50¢
   d. 12¢
   e. NH

7. Mary bought $1/4$ of a pound of coffee for $1.50. What was the cost per pound?

   a. $9.00
   b. $6.00
   c. $3.00
   d. 75¢
   e. NH

4. Matt bought $1/2$ of a gallon of gas for 60¢. What was the cost per gallon?

   f. $1.80
   g. $1.20
   h. 60¢
   j. 30¢
   k. NH

8. Tina paid $1.20 for $1/3$ of a pound of chocolate candy. What was the cost per pound?

   f. $3.60
   g. $2.40
   h. $1.20
   j. 40¢
   k. NH

Directions

Read each question and choose the correct answer. Mark the space for the answer you have hosen. Mark NH if the answer is not here.

1. Josh spent 50% of the $30 he had saved for a new CD. How much money did Josh spend?

   a. $10
   b. $15
   c. $20
   d. $25
   e. NH

2. In a recent election, Mike Jacob received 40% of the 1,500 votes cast. How many votes did he receive?

   f. 400
   g. 500
   h. 600
   j. 700
   k. NH

3. The class used 20% of their $400 treasury for student awards. How much money did they spend on awards?

   a. $80
   b. $120
   c. $140
   d. $160
   e. NH

4. 70% of the school voted to change the lunch room rules. If 600 children voted, how many wanted to change the lunch room rules?

   f. 420
   g. 300
   h. 180
   j. 42
   k. NH

5. If Hallie has saved $30 towards a new $50 cassette player, what percentage of the cost has she saved?

   a. 30%
   b. 40%
   c. 60%
   d. 80%
   e. NH

6. Kate Chavez was running for President of her eighth grade class. She received 60% of the 80 votes cast. How many votes did she receive?

   f. 24
   g. 36
   h. 48
   j. 60
   k. NH

7. The seventh grade class donated to charity 25% of the $80 they earned during a recycling drive. How much money did they donate to charity?

   a. $5
   b. $10
   c. $15
   d. $20
   e. NH

8. In one year, Lacey earned 10% interest on her $150 investment. How much money did she earn?

   f. $15
   g. $20
   h. $25
   j. $30
   k. NH

Name _____   Skill: Assessing Information

Directions
Read each question and choose the correct answer. Mark the space for the answer you have chosen. Mark NH if the answer is not here.

1. Jose bought 2 pounds of candy for a party. What else do you need to know to find out how much each pound of candy cost?

   a. the number of party guests
   b. the change he received
   c. the kind of candy he bought
   d. the cost of the 2 pounds of candy
   e. NH

2. Adriana spent 40% of her savings on clothes. What else do you need to know to find out how much money Adriana spent?

   f. the size she wears
   g. where she shopped
   h. if the items were on sale
   j. the amount of her savings
   k. NH

3. Ray bought 1/4 of a pound of jelly beans. What else must you know to find out the cost per pound?

   a. the kind of candy he bought
   b. how much he spent on 1/4 pound
   c. the number of jelly beans in a pound
   d. the color of the jelly beans
   e. NH

4. Mr. Smith drove 60 miles per hour. What else do you need to know to find out how far he traveled?

   f. the kind of car he drove
   g. how long he drove at that speed
   h. the time of day he drove
   j. where he was going
   k. NH

5. Bonnie is taking a 600-mile train trip. The train carries 310 passengers and averages 55 mph. It makes 3 fifteen-minute stops. What piece of information is not needed to find out how long the trip will take?

   a. 600 miles
   b. 55 miles per hour
   c. 3 fifteen-minute stops
   d. 310 passengers
   e. NH

6. A bike cost $150 and a radio costs $35. Jeff earns $20 a week. He has saved 50% of his earnings to buy the bike. What information is not needed to find out how much longer Jeff must save to buy the bike?

   f. the cost of the bike
   g. what he earns each week
   h. the percent he has saved
   j. the cost of the radio
   k. NH

7. Raisins cost $1.75 a pound, cashews cost $4.25, and peanuts cost $2.00. We want to mix the cashews and peanuts at a ratio of 3 to 1. What information is not needed to find out the cost of 4 pounds of the mixed nuts?

   a. the cost of the cashews
   b. the cost of the raisins
   c. the cost of the peanuts
   d. the ratio of cashew to peanuts
   e. NH

8. There are 210 eighth graders at the Middle School. 80% of them voted to buy a new computer. 20% voted for a field trip. What information is not needed to find out how many students voted for the computer?

   f. 80% voted for the computer
   g. 20% voted for the field trip
   h. there are 210 students
   j. the students are eighth graders
   k. NH

© Carson Dellosa CD-3757   84

Directions

Read each question and choose the correct answer. Mark the space for the answer you have chosen. Mark NH if the answer is not here.

1. Joey worked from 8:30 a.m. until 3:30 p.m. How many hours did he work?

 a. 5 hours
 b. 6 hours
 c. 7 hours
 d. 8 hours
 e. NH

2. The movie started at 2:05 p.m. and ended at 4:35 p.m. How long did the movie last?

 f. 2 hours
 g. 2 hours 30 minutes
 h. 3 hours 40 minutes
 j. 3 hours
 k. NH

3. The mall opens at 10 a.m. and closes at 9 p.m. How many hours is the mall open for business?

 a. 11 hours
 b. 10 hours
 c. 12 hours
 d. 13 hours
 e. NH

4. A fast food restaurant serves breakfast from 6:30 a.m. until 10:30 a.m. How long is breakfast served?

 f. 3 hours
 g. 4 hours
 h. 5 hours
 j. 6 hours
 k. NH

5. Our bus leaves at 2:30 p.m. It takes us 40 minutes to drive to the bus station, 5 minutes to park and 10 minutes to check in. What time should we leave our house?

 a. 1:35 p.m.
 b. 1:30 p.m.
 c. 1:25 p.m.
 d. 1:20 p.m.
 e. NH

6. The baseball game started at 2:30 p.m. If it lasted 3 hours and 15 minutes, what time did the game end?

 f. 5:30 p.m.
 g. 5:45 p.m.
 h. 6:00 p.m.
 j. 6:15 p.m.
 k. NH

7. Mom put the roast in the oven at 4:00 p.m. If it takes 2 hours and 45 minutes to cook, what time will the roast be ready?

 a. 5:45 p.m.
 b. 6:15 p.m.
 c. 6:30 p.m.
 d. 6:45 p.m.
 e. NH

8. The play starts at 7:00 p.m. Act I takes 45 minutes. Act II takes one hour and 10 minutes. There is a 15-minute intermission between acts. What time will the play end?

 f. 8:55 p.m.
 g. 9:05 p.m.
 h. 9:10 p.m.
 j. 9:15 p.m.
 k. NH

Directions

Read each question and choose the correct answer. Mark the space for the answer you have chosen. Mark NH if the answer is not here.

---

1. Joey played football from 3:45 p.m. until 5:45 p.m. How many hours did he play?

   a. 1 hour
   b. 2 hours
   c. 3 hours
   d. 4 hours
   e. NH

5. The play starts at 12:15 p.m. It takes us 20 minutes to drive to the theater and 25 minutes to park, get our tickets, and find a seat. What time should we leave our house?

   a. 1:35 a.m.
   b. 11:30 a.m.
   c. 10:30 a.m.
   d. 11:30 p.m.
   e. NH

---

2. The movie starts at 3:30 p.m. and lasts 63 minutes. What time will the movie end?

   f. 5:33 p.m.
   g. 4:30 p.m.
   h. 6:24 p.m.
   j. 5:45 p.m.
   k. NH

6. If my class starts at 1:45 p.m. and lasts 45 minutes, what time will my class end?

   f. 2:30 p.m.
   g. 2:45 p.m.
   h. 1:00 p.m.
   j. 6:15 p.m.
   k. NH

---

3. Sue can run a mile in 8 minutes. If she starts running at 2:12 p.m. and runs at this rate for three miles, what time will she finish running?

   a. 2:45 p.m.
   b. 2:52 p.m.
   c. 2:30 p.m.
   d. 2:36 p.m.
   e. NH

7. Maria is making a cake that she is supposed to bake for 35 minutes. If she starts baking at 11:45 a.m., what time will the cake be finished baking?

   a. 12:20 a.m.
   b. 12:20 p.m.
   c. 12:25 p.m.
   d. 11:55 a.m.
   e. NH

---

4. If Patty starts her homework at 2:45 p.m. and finishes at 4:55 p.m., how long will she have spent doing homework?

   f. 5 hours and seventeen minutes
   g. 2 hours and ten minutes
   h. 3 hours and ten minutes
   j. 2 hours
   k. NH

8. Bob left his house at 8:30 a.m. He spent 4 minutes in line at a fast food restaurant, 2 minutes at a red light, and drove a total of 25 minutes. What time did Bob arrive at school?

   f. 8:55 a.m.
   g. 9:05 a.m.
   h. 9:01 a.m.
   j. 9:00 a.m.
   k. NH

Directions
Read each question and choose the correct answer. Mark the space for the answer you have chosen. Mark NH if the answer is not here.

1. 1 meter =

    a. **10 centimeters**
    b. **100 centimeters**
    c. **100 millimeters**
    d. **100 kilometers**
    e. **NH**

5. 10 milligrams =

    a. **1 centigram**
    b. **100 centigrams**
    c. **100 grams**
    d. **100 grams**
    e. **NH**

2. 1 kilogram =

    f. **1 centigram**
    g. **1 milligram**
    h. **1,000 grams**
    j. **100 grams**
    k. **NH**

6. 1,000 meters =

    f. **10 centimeters**
    g. **1 millimeter**
    h. **10 kilometers**
    j. **1 kilometer**
    k. **NH**

3. 1,000 milliliters =

    a. **110 liters**
    b. **1 liter**
    c. **10 centiliters**
    d. **1 kiloliter**
    e. **NH**

7. 100 grams =

    a. **1 kilogram**
    b. **10,000 milligrams**
    c. **10,000 centigrams**
    d. **1 centigram**
    e. **NH**

4. 100 centimeters =

    f. **1 kilometer**
    g. **10 meters**
    h. **100 hectometers**
    j. **1,000 millimeters**
    k. **NH**

8. 1 centimeter =

    f. **1 millimeter**
    g. **10 millimeters**
    h. **100 meters**
    j. **1,000 meters**
    k. **NH**

Name _____

Directions
Read each question and choose the correct answer. Mark the space for the answer you have chosen. Mark NH if the answer is not here.

1. 2,000 meters equals how many kilometers?

    a. 2
    b. 20
    c. 0.2
    d. 200
    e. NH

5. 82 meters equals how many millimeters?

    a. 0.082
    b. 82
    c. 82,000
    d. 820
    e. NH

2. How many liters equal 6,000 milliliters?

    f. 0.6
    g. 6
    h. 60
    j. 600
    k. NH

6. 700 centimeters equals how many millimeters?

    f. 7
    g. 70
    h. 7,000
    j. 70.000
    k. NH

3. How many meters are in 5 kilometers?

    a. 5,000
    b. 500
    c. 50
    d. 0.005
    e. NH

7. Three kilograms equals how many grams?

    a. 30,000
    b. 3,000
    c. 300
    d. 30
    e. NH

4. 40 grams equals how many centigrams?

    f. 4
    g. 400
    h. 4,000
    j. 40,000
    k. NH

8. How many kilometers equal 5,200 meters?

    f. 5,200,000
    g. 520
    h. 52
    j. 5.2
    k. NH

Name _____

Directions

Use the graph to answer the questions. Read each question and choose the correct answer. Mark the space for the answer you have chosen. Mark NH if the answer is not here.

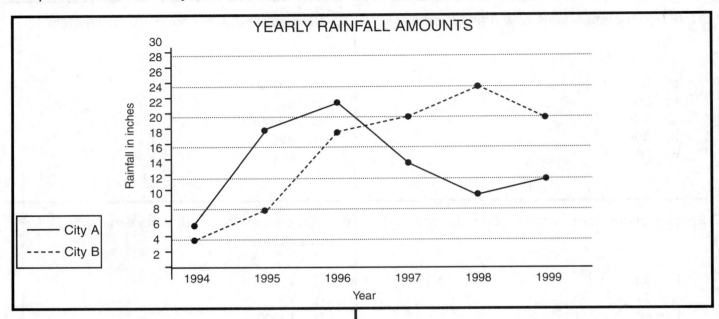

1. How many inches of rainfall did City A receive in 1995?

  a. **8 in**
  b. **12 in**
  c. **14 in**
  d. **18 in**
  e. **NH**

2. City B received approximately 18 inches of rain in which year?

  f. **1994**
  g. **1995**
  h. **1996**
  j. **1997**
  k. **NH**

3. In which year did both City A and City B receive the least rainfall?

  a. **1997**
  b. **1999**
  c. **1994**
  d. **1995**
  e. **NH**

4. In which year did City B receive about 14 inches more rainfall than City A?

  f. **1998**
  g. **1999**
  h. **1995**
  j. **1997**
  k. **NH**

5. City A received about 22 inches of rainfall in which year?

  a. **1994**
  b. **1996**
  c. **1995**
  d. **1998**
  e. **NH**

6. How many inches of rainfall did City A and City B receive together in 1998?

  f. **10 in**
  g. **18 in**
  h. **24 in**
  j. **34 in**
  k. **NH**

Name _____

Directions
Use the graph to answer the questions. Read each question and choose the correct answer. Mark the space for the answer you have chosen. Mark NH if the answer is not here.

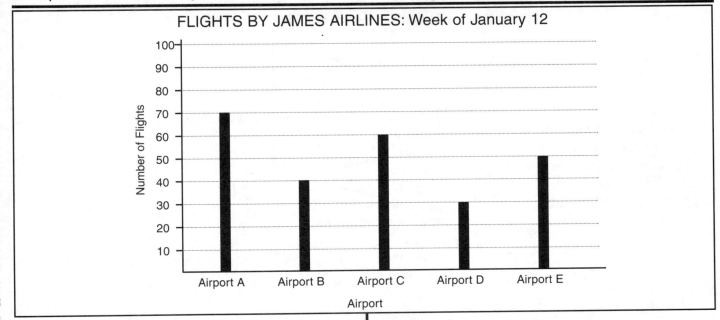

FLIGHTS BY JAMES AIRLINES: Week of January 12

1. To which airport did James Airlines make the least number of flights during that week?

   a. A
   b. B
   c. C
   d. D
   e. NH

2. How many more flights did James Airlines have to Airport C than Airport B?

   f. 10
   g. 20
   h. 30
   j. 40
   k. NH

3. Which airport had as many flights as Airports D and B added together?

   a. D
   b. C
   c. B
   d. A
   e. NH

4. How many flights did the airline make to Airports A and D during this week?

   f. 60
   g. 80
   h. 95
   j. 120
   k. NH

5. The number of flights made to Airports A and D is the same as the number of flights between which 2 airports?

   a. B and D
   b. B and C
   c. C and E
   d. D and E
   e. NH

6. What was the total number of flights shown on this graph during that week?

   f. 300
   g. 250
   h. 200
   j. 150
   k. NH

Name _____

Directions
Use the graph to answer the questions. Read each question and choose the correct answer. Mark the space for the answer you have chosen. Mark NH if the answer is not here.

FAVORITE FAST FOODS

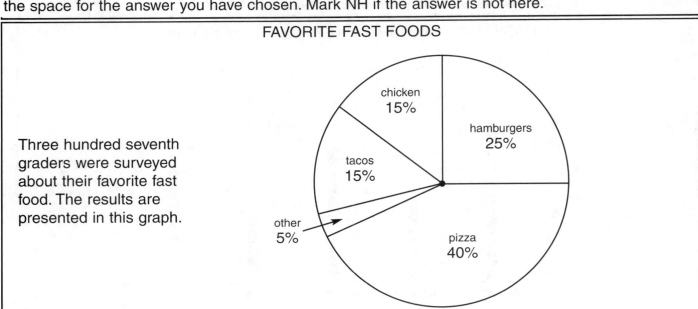

Three hundred seventh graders were surveyed about their favorite fast food. The results are presented in this graph.

1. How many people voted pizza as their favorite fast food?

   a. 40
   b. 80
   c. 120
   d. 160
   e. NH

2. How many people chose hamburgers as their favorite fast food?

   f. 15
   g. 25
   h. 50
   j. 75
   k. NH

3. How many more people chose hamburgers than tacos as their favorite fast food?

   a. 10
   b. 30
   c. 50
   d. 70
   e. NH

4. How many people chose either chicken or tacos as their favorite fast food?

   f. 90
   g. 60
   h. 45
   j. 30
   k. NH

5. How many more people chose pizza than chicken?

   a. 120
   b. 75
   c. 60
   d. 40
   e. NH

6. How many people <u>did not</u> choose tacos as their favorite fast food?

   f. 300
   g. 180
   h. 255
   j. 295
   k. NH

Name _____

Directions

Use the frequency table to answer the questions. Read each question and choose the correct answer. Mark the space for the answer you have chosen. Mark NH if the answer is not here.

The following table shows the number of students earning different scores on an English exam.

ENGLISH EXAM SCORES	
Score	**Frequency**
100	1
96	5
92	1
88	3
82	4
78	8
72	2
68	3
64	1
60	2

1. How many students took the exam?

   a. 25
   b. 26
   c. 28
   d. 30
   e. NH

2. How many students scored 96 or higher?

   f. 5
   g. 6
   h. 7
   j. 8
   k. NH

3. What percentage of students taking the test scored 68 or below?

   a. 6%
   b. 10%
   c. 20%
   d. 40%
   e. NH

4. How many students scored between 80 and 90?

   f. 7
   g. 5
   h. 4
   j. 3
   k. NH

5. Which score had the highest frequency for this English exam?

   a. 96
   b. 82
   c. 68
   d. 64
   e. NH

6. Which score had the lowest frequency on this test?

   f. 96
   g. 82
   h. 68
   j. 64
   k. NH

7. How many students passed the test with a score of 80 or higher?

   a. 5
   b. 14
   c. 13
   d. 22
   e. NH

Name _____

Directions
Use the frequency table to answer the questions. Read each question and choose the correct answer. Mark the space for the answer you have chosen. Mark NH if the answer is not here.

Mr. Welby's seventh grade math class surveyed the entire student body to find the types of vacations that students prefer. The results are summarized in the following table:

FAVORITE VACATIONS	
Types	**Frequency**
Amusement Park	352
Camping	78
Historical Town	15
Relaxing (no specific plans)	32
Visiting Relatives	100
Water Sports (swimming, surfing, skiing, etc.)	215

1. How many students were surveyed?

   a. 872
   b. 726
   c. 782
   d. 792
   e. NH

2. How many students liked to visit relatives or historical towns?

   f. 115
   g. 0
   h. 352
   j. 792
   k. NH

3. How many students _do not_ prefer amusement park vacations?

   a. 352
   b. 430
   c. 440
   d. 450
   e. NH

4. How many students like to go camping for a vacation?

   f. 78
   g. 235
   h. 512
   j. 714
   k. NH

5. Which type of vacation had the highest frequency according to this survey?

   a. relaxing
   b. water sports
   c. amusement parks
   d. camping
   e. NH

6. Which vacation type had the lowest frequency of all the types on this survey?

   f. relaxing
   g. water sports
   h. amusements
   j. camping
   k. NH

7. How many students liked camping or visiting historical towns?

   a. 78
   b. 15
   c. 132
   d. 93
   e. NH

Directions

Use the frequency table to answer the questions. Read each question and choose the correct answer. Mark the space for the answer you have chosen. Mark NH if the answer is not here.

During a probability experiment, Kevin tossed a die 100 times. He kept a careful count of the number of times each number was rolled. The table below summarizes his findings.

KEVIN'S FREQUENCY TABLE	
Outcome	**Frequency**
1	15
2	14
3	24
4	16
5	8
6	23

1. How many times did Kevin roll a 2?

a. 24
b. 16
c. 14
d. 100
e. NH

2. How many times did Kevin roll a number less than 5?

f. 69
g. 77
h. 61
j. 31
k. NH

3. How many times did Kevin roll a 7?

a. 15
b. 14
c. 0
d. 100
e. NH

4. How many times did Kevin roll an even number?

f. 53
g. 47
h. 52
j. 48
k. NH

5. Which numbers were rolled more than 20 times each?

a. 1 and 3
b. 3 and 5
c. 3 and 4
d. 6 and 3
e. NH

6. Which number was rolled 16% of the time?

f. 2
g. 3
h. 4
j. 6
k. NH

7. How many times did Kevin roll an odd number?

a. 53
b. 47
c. 52
d. 48
e. NH

Directions

Use the table to answer the questions. Read each question and choose the correct answer. Mark the space for the answer you have chosen. Mark NH if the answer is not here.

This table shows the amount and type of items sold by Smart Books during 4 weeks in April.

SMART BOOKS—SALES IN APRIL

	Reference	Science Fiction	Novels	Biographies	Magazines
Week 1	111	91	150	87	189
Week 2	59	102	108	122	184
Week 3	78	121	137	101	147
Week 4	107	98	110	97	124

1. How many science fiction books were sold in the second week of April?

   a. 98
   b. 59
   c. 102
   d. 121
   e. NH

2. How many reference books were sold during April?

   f. 355
   g. 412
   h. 589
   j. 628
   k. NH

3. How many more novels than biographies were sold during the first week of April?

   a. 53
   b. 57
   c. 63
   d. 67
   e. NH

4. Which items sold the most in all of April?

   f. magazines
   g. biographies
   h. reference books
   j. science fiction
   k. NH

5. What was the total number of items sold during the third week of April?

   a. 527
   b. 584
   c. 618
   d. 645
   e. NH

6. What was the average number of science fiction books sold each week in April?

   f. 91
   g. 102
   h. 112
   j. 103
   k. NH

Directions
Use the table to answer the questions. Read each question and choose the correct answer. Mark the space for the answer you have chosen. Mark NH if the answer is not here.

CITY MARATHON

In this table, the winning time (in minutes) for the City Marathon is listed along with the year of the race.

Year	Winning Time
1992	228
1993	170
1994	169
1995	145
1996	152
1997	143
1998	127
1999	114

1. In which year was the winning time greater than that of the previous year?

   a. 1995
   b. 1996
   c. 1997
   d. 1998
   e. NH

2. By how many minutes did the winning time improve between 1994 and 1999?

   f. 45 minutes
   g. 50 minutes
   h. 55 minutes
   j. 60 minutes
   k. NH

3. Between which two consecutive years is the difference in winning times the greatest?

   a. 1992 and 1993
   b. 1994 and 1995
   c. 1997 and 1998
   d. 1998 and 1999
   e. NH

4. By what percent was the winning time reduced between 1992 and 1999?

   f. 40%
   g. 50%
   h. 60%
   j. 70%
   k. NH

5. What was the difference in the winning times of 1993 and 1994?

   a. 7 minutes
   b. 5 minutes
   c. 3 minutes
   d. 1 minute
   e. NH

6. By how many minutes did the winning time improve between 1995 and 1998?

   f. 18 minutes
   g. 16 minutes
   h. 10 minutes
   j. 2 minutes
   k. NH

Name _____

Skill: Table

Directions

Use the table to answer the questions. Read each question and choose the correct answer. Mark the space for the answer you have chosen. Mark NH if the answer is not here.

The votes in a seventh grade class student council election are summarized in this table.

Key: **o** = 10 votes

SEVENTH GRADE STUDENT COUNCIL ELECTION	
Candidate's Name	Votes
Samantha Aubert	o o o o o o (
Jack Kelley	o o o o (
Melody Lawless	o o o o o (
Andy Madison	o o o o o
Catherine Sampson	o o o o

1. How many votes did Melody Lawless receive?

a. 40
b. 45
c. 55
d. 60
e. NH

2. How many votes were cast in all?

f. 245
g. 255
h. 265
j. 275
k. NH

3. How many more votes did Samantha get than Catherine?

a. 10
b. 15
c. 25
d. 30
e. NH

4. How many more votes did the females receive than the males?

f. 65
g. 75
h. 80
j. 85
k. NH

5. How many less votes did Jack receive than Melody?

a. 5
b. 10
c. 15
d. 20
e. NH

6. What fraction of the votes did Andy receive?

f. $\frac{5}{11}$ j. $\frac{5}{51}$

g. $\frac{11}{50}$ k. NH

h. $\frac{15}{51}$

Directions
Use the table to answer the questions. Read each question and choose the correct answer. Mark the space for the answer you have chosen. Mark NH if the answer is not here.

This table contains the results of Mrs. Lavery's eighth grade pre-algebra exam.

PRE-ALGEBRA EXAM RESULTS

Exam Score	Number of Students
100	1
95	3
90	5
85	7
80	12
75	8
70	5
65	2
60	0
55	1
50	0

1. What is the mean (average) grade for the exam?

   a. 78
   b. 80
   c. 82
   d. 84
   e. NH

2. What is the mode (most common score) of this sample?

   f. 80
   g. 75
   h. 70
   j. 65
   k. NH

3. What is the median (middle) score for this exam?

   a. 80
   b. 85
   c. 90
   d. 95
   e. NH

4. What is the range (difference between the highest and lowest scores) of these exam grades?

   f. 55
   g. 50
   h. 45
   j. 40
   k. NH

5. How many students scored below an 80 on this exam?

   a. 22
   b. 20
   c. 18
   d. 16
   e. NH

6. What percentage of students scored an 85 or above on this exam?

   f. 31%
   g. 36%
   h. 41%
   j. 46%
   k. NH

Directions
Read each question and choose the correct answer. Mark the space for the answer you have chosen. Mark NH if the answer is not here.

---

1. Polly earns scores of 76, 87, and 92 on her three English tests. What is her average score on the tests?

   a. 85
   b. 80
   c. 83
   d. 84
   e. NH

5. Which angle measures 90°?

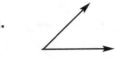

   e. NH

---

2. In one year, Vicki earned 15% interest on her $200 investment. How much money did she earn?

   f. $15
   g. $20
   h. $25
   j. $30
   k. NH

6. If you pick a month of the year at random, what is the probability that its name will start with the letter "N"?

   f. $\frac{4}{12}$ j. $\frac{1}{12}$

   g. $\frac{2}{12}$ k. NH

   h. $\frac{3}{12}$

---

3. 100 centimeters =

   a. 1 kilometer
   b. 10 meters
   c. 100 hectometers
   d. 1,000 millimeters
   e. NH

7. The fifth grade class donated to charity 40% of the $80 they earned during bake sale. How much money did they donate to charity?

   a. $32
   b. $40
   c. $60
   d. $20
   e. NH

---

4. Figures EFGH and IJKL are congruent. Which is a pair of corresponding angles?

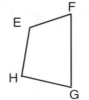
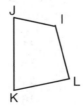

   f. ∠F and ∠L
   g. ∠F and ∠J
   h. ∠G and ∠J
   j. ∠H and ∠I
   k. NH

8. Which number sentence means, "the product of a number and 4 is 32"?

   f. $4 \div n = 32$
   g. $4 + n = 32$
   h. $4n = 32$
   j. $4 - n = 32$
   k. NH

Name _____

Directions

Read each question and choose the correct answer. Mark the space for the answer you have chosen. Mark NH if the answer is not here.

---

1. Andrea bought three packs of bubble gum for 32¢ each. If there is no tax, how much change will she receive from $1.00? Which number sentence can you use to find the answer?

   a. (0.32 x 3) – 1.00 = n
   b. 1.00 x (3 – 0.32) = n
   c. 3 – (1.00 x 0.32) = n
   d. 1.00 – (0.32 x 3) = n
   e. NH

5. Which equation means "15 more than 3 times a number is 21"?

   a. $3n - 15 = 21$
   b. $3n + 15 = 21$
   c. $3(n + 15) = 21$
   d. $3n + 21 = 15$
   e. NH

---

2. 1,000 meters equals how many kilometers?

   f. 1
   g. 10
   h. 0.1
   j. 100
   k. NH

6. George's savings account balance was $56.84. He deposited $184.12. What is his new balance?

   f. $35.23
   g. $256.87
   h. $240.96
   j. $225.41
   k. NH

---

3. Which word most accurately describes the following lines?

   a. **Parallel**
   b. **Intersecting**
   c. **Perpendicular**
   d. **Acute**
   e. **NH**

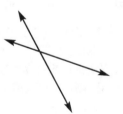

7. What is the area of this rectangle in square inches?

   a. 18 in^2
   b. 12 in^2
   c. 9 in^2
   d. 36 in^2
   e. NH

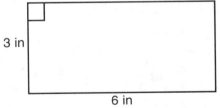

---

4. The movie we went to see started at 2:35 and ended at 4:15. How long was the movie?

   f. **45 minutes**
   g. **2 hours and 40 minutes**
   h. **1 hour and 40 minutes**
   j. **1 hour and 45 minutes**
   k. **NH**

8. What is the measure of angle ACB given the following:
   • Angle ABC = 113°
   • Angle BAC = 35°

   f. 22°
   g. 32°
   h. 42°
   j. 52°
   k. NH

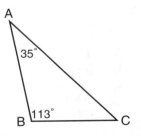

Directions

Read each question and choose the correct answer. Mark the space for the answer you have chosen. Mark NH if the answer is not here.

---

1. Which point is located at (3, − 2)?

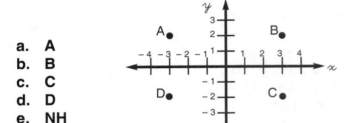

   a. **A**
   b. **B**
   c. **C**
   d. **D**
   e. **NH**

5. At the class bake sale we sold 15 cookies at 45¢ each, 12 cupcakes at 60¢ each and 5 pies at $3.75 each. How much did we make?

   a. **$28.95**
   b. **$37.20**
   c. **$32.70**
   d. **$25.63**
   e. **NH**

---

2. What is the perimeter of this trapezoid?

   f. **20 m**
   g. **38 m**
   h. **28 m**
   j. **18 m**
   k. **NH**

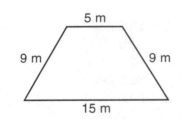

6. A hamburger costs $3.95, fries are $1.25, and a drink is 90¢. How much will it cost to get a lunch consisting of all three items?

   f. **$5.69**
   g. **$5.96**
   h. **$6.00**
   j. **$6.10**
   k. **NH**

---

3. A bag contains 3 red balls, 5 green balls, and 5 yellow balls. What is the probability that a ball you choose at random will be yellow?

   a. $\frac{4}{13}$ d. $\frac{5}{13}$

   b. $\frac{1}{13}$ e. **NH**

   c. $\frac{3}{13}$

7. Rodney bought 8 pieces of pie at 85¢ each. How much change did he receive from a $10 bill? (There was no tax.) Which number sentence can you use to find the answer?

   a. **10.00 − (8 x 0.85) = n**
   b. **(10.00 − 8) x 0.85 = n**
   c. **(8 x 0.85) + 10.00 = n**
   d. **0.85 − (10.00 ÷ 8) = n**
   e. **NH**

---

4. Which of the following is a radius of the circle?

   f. $\overline{JK}$
   g. $\overline{JL}$
   h. $\overline{KH}$
   j. $\overline{KL}$
   k. **NH**

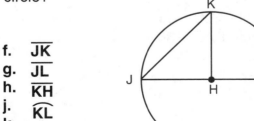

8. Which angle is obtuse?

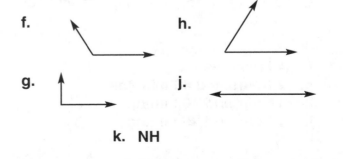

   k. **NH**

Name _____

Directions

Read each question and choose the correct answer. Mark the space for the answer you have chosen. Mark NH if the answer is not here.

---

1. Which of the following is a chord of the circle?

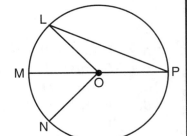

  a. $\overline{LN}$
  b. $\overline{NO}$
  c. $\overline{LO}$
  d. $\overline{LP}$
  e. NH

5. An elevator stopped on the 20th floor. It went down 11 floors and then back up 5 floors. At what floor is the elevator now?

  a. 10
  b. 14
  c. 12
  d. 13
  e. NH

---

2. If Chris paid 45¢ for $^{1}/_{3}$ pound of grapes, how much would 1 pound have cost?

  f. 90¢
  g. $1.35
  h. $1.45
  j. $1.05
  k. NH

6. Which word most accurately describes the following lines?

  f. **Parallel**
  g. **Intersecting**
  h. **Perpendicular**
  j. **Acute**
  k. **NH**

---

3. Pam bought two pairs of socks at $5.99 each and a bracelet that was $18.50. The tax on the two items was $1.71. What was the total?

  a. $24.49
  b. $21.25
  c. $24.15
  d. $26.20
  e. NH

7. Our school play starts at 4.30 p.m. If it lasts 90 minutes, what time will it end?

  a. 5:30 p.m.
  b. 5:45 p.m.
  c. 6:00 p.m.
  d. 6:15 p.m.
  e. NH

---

4. 30 grams equals how many centigrams?

  f. **3**
  g. **300**
  h. **3,000**
  j. **30,000**
  k. **NH**

8. Which of the following could not be the measurement of an acute angle?

  f. **123°**
  g. **67°**
  h. **55°**
  j. **11.8°**
  k. **NH**

Name _____

Directions
Read each question and choose the correct answer. Mark the space for the answer you have chosen. Mark NH if the answer is not here.

---

1. Rollins had $80. He spent half of it on a new video game. How much did he spend?

   a. $40
   b. $20
   c. $50
   d. $30
   e. NH

2. John rode his bike 15 miles to his friend's house and averaged 10 minutes per mile. What else do you need to know to find out what time he arrived?

   f. the kind of bike he rode
   g. what kind of mood John was in
   h. the time that he left
   j. what John ate for breakfast
   k. NH

3. Mark read seven books in May, seven books in June, and 10 books in July. What is the average number of books that he read per month?

   a. 7
   b. 8
   c. 9
   d. 10
   e. NH

4. Name the figure shown below.

   f. Circle MN
   g. Circle A
   h. Circle MAN
   j. Circle N
   k. NH

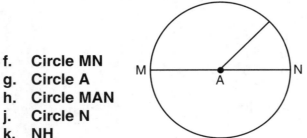

5. Figures RST and UVW are congruent. Which is a pair of corresponding angles?

   a. ∠R and ∠W
   b. ∠S and ∠U
   c. ∠T and ∠W
   d. ∠V and ∠T
   e. NH

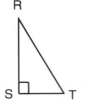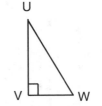

6. What is the name of the following?

   f. Line RS
   g. Ray RS
   h. Line Segment RS
   j. Angle RS
   k. NH

7. 1 centimeter =

   a. 1 millimeter
   b. 10 millimeters
   c. 100 meters
   d. 1,000 meters
   e. NH

8. At which point does $x = -3$ and $y = 2$?

   f. A
   g. B
   h. C
   j. D
   k. NH

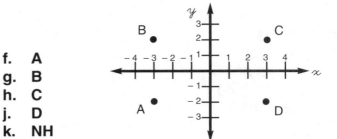

Directions

Read each question and choose the correct answer. Mark the space for the answer you have chosen. Mark NH if the answer is not here.

---

1. What is the measure of angle LNM given the following:

   Angle LMN = 90°
   Angle MLN = 45°

   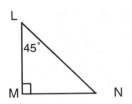

   a. 65°
   b. 55°
   c. 45°
   d. 35°
   e. NH

5. Which number sentence means, "ten more than 3 times a number is 25"?

   a. 3(n +10) = 25
   b. (3 ÷ n) + 10 = 25
   c. 10 ÷ 3n = 25
   d. 3n + 10 = 25
   e. NH

---

2. What is the volume of this cube in cubic feet?

   f. 10 ft³
   g. 100 ft³
   h. 1,000 ft³
   j. 10,000 ft³
   k. NH

   10 ft

6. Calvin spent 85% of his birthday money at the music store. What else do you need to know to find out how much money Calvin spent?

   f. the type of music he likes
   g. the amount of his savings
   h. how many items he purchased
   j. how many stores he went to
   k. NH

---

3. Frank has $25 saved toward the $100 bike he wants. What fraction of the cost of the bike does he have now?

   a. $\frac{3}{4}$ d. $\frac{1}{4}$

   b. $\frac{1}{3}$ e. NH

   c. $\frac{1}{2}$

7. Which of the following figures illustrates Line EF?

   e. NH

---

4. At which point does x = 3 and y = 2?

   f. A
   g. B
   h. C
   j. D
   k. NH

   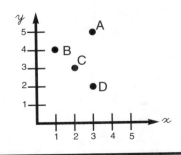

8. Paul bought four goldfish. Each fish cost .89¢. How much did he spend on the fish?

   f. $3.56
   g. $2.34
   h. $3.15
   j. $1.23
   k. NH

Directions
Use the frequency table to answer the questions. Read each question and choose the correct answer. Mark the space for the answer you have chosen. Mark NH if the answer is not here.

The following table shows the favorite sports of the seventh-grade class.

FAVORITE SPORTS CHART	
Favorite Sport	**Frequency**
Soccer	5
Football	5
Baseball	8
Basketball	7
Track	4
Hockey	1
Volleyball	2
Swimming	3
Tennis	2
Golf	3

3. What is the most preferred sport?

   a. football
   b. baseball
   c. volleyball
   d. swimming
   e. NH

4. What is the least preferred sport?

   f. football
   g. hockey
   h. volleyball
   j. swimming
   k. NH

5. What percentage of students prefer soccer, swimming, or tennis?

   a. 20%
   b. 25%
   c. 30%
   d. 50%
   e. NH

1. How many students are in the seventh grade?

   a. 25
   b. 40
   c. 36
   d. 30
   e. NH

2. How many students prefer soccer or track?

   f. 5
   g. 6
   h. 7
   j. 8
   k. NH

6. How many students preferred volleyball, golf, and basketball in all?

   f. 10
   g. 5
   h. 12
   j. 9
   k. NH

7. How many sports are preferred by at least 4 students?

   a. 5
   b. 4
   c. 7
   d. 6
   e. NH

Directions

Use the table to answer the questions. Read each question and choose the correct answer. Mark the space for the answer you have chosen. Mark NH if the answer is not here.

This table shows the number and type of music purchased from Mario's Music Ranch in a six-month period.

Mario's Music Ranch (six-month sales)						
	Country	Rock	Classical	Oldies	Pop	Soul
January	101	57	48	87	156	111
February	125	60	52	81	178	104
March	94	75	75	82	152	98
April	87	58	49	74	186	125
May	112	52	71	74	149	109
June	115	63	85	78	174	113

1. In April, how many more pop recordings were sold than country?

   a. 45
   b. 55
   c. 65
   d. 58
   e. NH

2. In June, what type of music was purchased most?

   f. pop
   g. oldies
   h. rock
   j. country
   k. NH

3. How many soul recordings were purchased during this six-month period?

   a. 698
   b. 556
   c. 660
   d. 542
   e. NH

4. During which month did Mario's Music Ranch sell the most recordings?

   f. March
   g. January
   h. May
   j. June
   k. NH

5. What is the average number of recordings sold each month?

   a. 585
   b. 497
   c. 560
   d. 485
   e. NH

6. Approximately what percent of the recordings sold in March were oldies?

   f. 30%
   g. 20%
   h. 10%
   j. 14%
   k. NH

Name _____

Directions

Read each question and choose the correct answer. Mark the space for the answer you have chosen. Mark NH if the answer is not here.

1. What is the numeral for three million, sixty-two thousand, five?

    a. 3,006,201
    b. 36,200,005
    c. 3,620,005
    d. 3,062,005
    e. NH

2. Which is another way of writing 11 + (3 + 2)?

    f. 11 + (3 + 5)
    g. (11 + 3) + 5
    h. (11 + 3) + 2
    j. 11 + (3 + 6)
    k. NH

3. Which is another name for 9?

    a. $18 \div 2 + 7$
    b. $3 + (24 \div 4)$
    c. $12 - (16 \div 8)$
    d. $27 \div 3 - 2$
    e. NH

4. What decimal is another name for $5 \frac{3}{4}$?

    f. 0.575
    g. 5.75
    h. 57.5
    j. 575
    k. NH

5. What does the 7 in 5,070,164 represent?

    a. 7,000
    b. 700,000
    c. 70,000
    d. 700
    e. NH

6. What number is one tenth more than 128.5?

    f. 138.5
    g. 129.5
    h. 128.6
    j. 129.6
    k. NH

7. What is 815,062.1 rounded to the nearest hundred?

    a. 815,000
    b. 815,100
    c. 815,060
    d. 815,062
    e. NH

8. What is the least common denominator for $\frac{1}{2}$, $\frac{5}{7}$, and $\frac{3}{14}$?

    f. 14
    g. 28
    h. 98
    j. 196
    k. NH

9. Which fraction names the smallest number?

    a. $\frac{5}{8}$ d. $\frac{7}{13}$

    b. $\frac{3}{12}$ e. NH

    c. $\frac{3}{8}$

10. Which fraction is in its simplest form?

    f. $\frac{5}{18}$ j. $\frac{15}{24}$

    g. $\frac{2}{24}$ k. NH

    h. $\frac{9}{15}$

Name _____

Directions

Read each question and choose the correct answer. Mark the space for the answer you have chosen. Mark NH if the answer is not here.

---

1. 6 x 668 =

   a. 3,708
   b. 3,966
   c. 3,996
   d. 4,008
   e. NH

6. Estimate the answer by rounding:
   5.307 x 9.93

   f. 53
   g. 50
   h. 47
   j. 40
   k. NH

---

2. 1674 ÷ 3 =

   f. 588
   g. 585
   h. 578
   j. 558
   k. NH

7. Estimate the answer by rounding:
   59.879 ÷ 11.9

   a. 7
   b. 6
   c. 5
   d. 4
   e. NH

---

3. 8046 ÷ 90 is between which numbers?

   a. 60 and 70
   b. 70 and 80
   c. 80 and 90
   d. 90 and 100
   e. NH

8. Estimate the answer by rounding:
   62.54 ÷ 8.324

   f. 8
   g. 7
   h. 6
   j. 5
   k. NH

---

4. 3.1 + 5.2 + 1.2 =

   f. 9.2
   g. 9.5
   h. 9.6
   j. 9.9
   k. NH

9. $\frac{4}{5} + \frac{8}{9} =$

   a. $1\frac{30}{45}$ d. $1\frac{2}{5}$

   b. $1\frac{31}{45}$ e. NH

   c. $2\frac{1}{4}$

---

5. 72.05 − 49.996 =

   a. 22.054
   b. 22.991
   c. 23.904
   d. 23.894
   e. NH

10. $\frac{7}{8} - \frac{2}{3} =$

   f. $\frac{5}{24}$ j. $\frac{1}{2}$

   g. $\frac{1}{6}$ k. NH

   h. $\frac{1}{4}$

Directions

Read each question and choose the correct answer. Mark the space for the answer you have chosen. Mark NH if the answer is not here.

1. The temperature five hours ago was 3°F. In the past hour it has dropped 6°. What is the temperature now?

   a.   9°
   b.   3°
   c.   − 3°
   d.   − 6°
   e.   NH

2. Jackie had $23.45 in her pocket. She spent $3.15 on ice cream and $4.98 on a taxi. Then she bought a tie for $12.15. How much money does she have left?

   f. $4.27
   g. $3.27
   h. $2.17
   j. $3.17
   k.   NH

3. Kendra bought a pie for $3.96. Tax was 32¢. How much change did Kendra receive from a $20 bill?

   a. $15.72
   b. $5.72
   c. $16.04
   d. $15.81
   e.   NH

4. Stereo A costs $79.50, but Stereo B is on sale for $54.95. How much less does Stereo B cost than Stereo A?

   f. $34.50
   g. $24.50
   h. $24.55
   j. $24.45
   k.   NH

5. Jessie bowled three games. Her scores were 94, 106, and 124. What was her average score for the three games?

   a.   40
   b.   108
   c.   110
   d.   111
   e.   NH

6. The recipe calls for 6 eggs to every one cup of milk. If the chef uses 42 eggs, how many cups of milk will be needed?

   f.   5
   g.   6
   h.   6.5
   j.   8
   k.   NH

7. If you have 3 red marbles and 6 green marbles in a bag, what is the probability that you will pull out a red marble?

   a. $\frac{3}{6}$ d. $\frac{3}{9}$

   b. $\frac{6}{3}$ e. NH

   c. $\frac{1}{9}$

8. Carlos bought 12 pencils at 10¢ apiece. No tax was charged. How much change did he get from a $10 bill?

   f. $9.20
   g. $8.80
   h. $8.20
   j. $7.20
   k.   NH

Directions
Read each question and choose the correct answer. Mark the space for the answer you have chosen. Mark NH if the answer is not here.

1. Which is a pair of prime numbers?

   a. (2, 15)
   b. (7, 13)
   c. (3, 8)
   d. (4, 9)
   e. NH

6. $4^3 =$

   f. 12
   g. 81
   h. 36
   j. 64
   k. NH

2. What is the prime factorization of 50?

   f. 5 x 10
   g. 5 x 5 x 10
   h. 25 x 2
   j. 2 x 5 x 5
   k. NH

7. What fraction is another name for $\frac{2}{5}$?

   a. $\frac{4}{25}$ d. $\frac{8}{25}$

   b. $\frac{8}{20}$ e. NH

   c. $\frac{4}{20}$

3. Which numbers are in order from least to greatest?

   a. 4, – 3, – 5
   b. – 5, – 3, 4
   c. – 3, – 5, 4
   d. – 3, 4, – 5
   e. NH

8. Which is another name for 8?

   f. (5 x 2) –2
   g. 3 + (15 ÷ 5)
   h. 17 – (27 ÷ 9)
   j. 12 ÷ 3 + 5
   k. NH

4. 12 + (– 8) =

   f. 5
   g. 4
   h. – 3
   j. – 5
   k. NH

9. What is the numeral for fourteen million, one hundred three?

   a. 14,103
   b. 14,000,103
   c. 1,400,103
   d. 14,103,000
   e. NH

5. The "n" stands for what number?
   2 x (5 + n) = (2 x 5) + (2 x 1)

   a. 12
   b. 5
   c. 2
   d. 1
   e. NH

10. Which is another way of writing 10 x (3 + 4)?

   f. (10 x 3) x (10 x 4)
   g. (10 x 3) + (10 x 4)
   h. (10 x 3) + 4
   j. 10 x (3 + 7)
   k. NH

Directions

Read each question and choose the correct answer. Mark the space for the answer you have chosen. Mark NH if the answer is not here.

---

1. $\frac{3}{4} \times \frac{4}{9} =$

    a. $\frac{2}{3}$ d. $\frac{5}{6}$

    b. $\frac{1}{3}$ e. NH

    c. $\frac{1}{6}$

6. 8 is 10% of what number?

    f. 880
    g. 80
    h. 88
    j. 800
    k. NH

---

2. $2\frac{1}{4} \times \frac{2}{3} =$

    f. $1\frac{1}{2}$ j. $2\frac{1}{4}$

    g. $1\frac{2}{3}$ k. NH

    h. $2\frac{1}{6}$

7. 4 is what percent of 40?

    a. 4%
    b. 5%
    c. 10%
    d. 25%
    e. NH

---

3. $\frac{3}{7} \div \frac{4}{5} =$

    a. $\frac{12}{35}$ d. $\frac{3}{4}$

    b. $1\frac{11}{12}$ e. NH

    c. $\frac{15}{28}$

8. If $n + 5 = 12$, then $n =$

    f. 7
    g. 6
    h. 5
    j. 4
    k. NH

---

4. $3\frac{3}{5} \div 4\frac{1}{2} =$

    f. $\frac{4}{5}$ j. $\frac{3}{10}$

    g. $1\frac{1}{5}$ k. NH

    h. $1\frac{1}{4}$

9. If $n - 4 = 6$, then $n =$

    a. 9
    b. 10
    c. 11
    d. 12
    e. NH

---

5. 7% of 300 =

    a. 210
    b. 2.1
    c. 21
    d. 0.21
    e. NH

10. If $2n = 22$, then $n =$

    f. 9
    g. 10
    h. 11
    j. 12
    k. NH

Name _____

Directions

Read each question and choose the correct answer. Mark the space for the answer you have chosen. Mark NH if the answer is not here.

---

1. Which number sentence means "the quotient of a number and − 4 is 24"?

  a. $n \div (-4) = 24$
  b. $(-4) - n = 24$
  c. $-4 \times n = 24$
  d. $n + (-4) = 24$
  e. NH

2. Which angle measures 90°?

  f.    h.

  g. 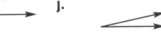   j.

            k. NH

3. What is the measure of an obtuse angle?

  a. **exactly 90°**
  b. **less than 180°**
  c. **between 90° and 180°**
  d. **less than 90°**
  e. **NH**

4. What is the measure of angle ABC given:

  Angle CAB = 70°
  Angle ACB = 50°

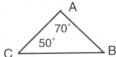

  f. **50°**
  g. **60°**
  h. **70°**
  j. **80°**
  k. **NH**

---

5. If the measure of radius $\overline{OP}$ is 8 cm, what is the measure of $\overline{OM}$?

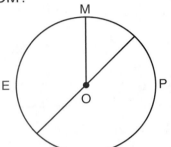

  a. **12 cm**
  b. **8 cm**
  c. **6 cm**
  d. **3 cm**
  e. **NH**

6. What is the perimeter of this parallelogram?

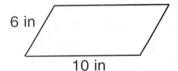

  f. **16 in**
  g. **32 in**
  h. **26 in**
  j. **60 in**
  k. **NH**

7. A rectangular board is 6 feet wide and 12 feet long. What is the area of the board in square feet?

  a. 18 ft^2
  b. 40 ft^2
  c. 36 ft^2
  d. 72 ft^2
  e. **NH**

8. What is the volume of this prism in cubic millimeters?

  f. 160 mm^3
  g. 400 mm^3
  h. 40 mm^3
  j. 72 mm^3
  k. **NH**

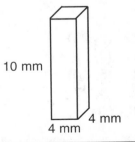

Directions

Read each question and choose the correct answer. Mark the space for the answer you have chosen. Mark NH if the answer is not here.

---

1. Which fraction is another name for $\frac{3}{5}$?

   a. $\frac{6}{10}$ d. $\frac{9}{10}$

   b. $\frac{9}{25}$ e. NH

   c. $\frac{6}{25}$

6. What is the prime factorization of 90?

   f. **9 x 10**
   g. **2 x 3 x 3 x 5**
   h. **2 x 45**
   j. **6 x 15**
   k. **NH**

---

2. The 9 in 0.109845 represents ...

   f. **9 thousandths**
   g. **9 ten thousandths**
   h. **9 hundredths**
   j. **9 tenths**
   k. **NH**

7. Which numbers are in order from least to greatest?

   a. **− 8, − 10, − 2**
   b. **− 2, − 8, − 10**
   c. **− 10, − 2, − 8**
   d. **− 10, − 8, − 2**
   e. **NH**

---

3. What is 5,625 rounded to the nearest thousand?

   a. **5,000**
   b. **6,000**
   c. **5,600**
   d. **5,630**
   e. **NH**

8. $10 \times (- 8) =$

   f. **− 80**
   g. **2**
   h. **80**
   j. **18**
   k. **NH**

---

4. What is the least common denominator for $\frac{2}{3}$, $\frac{5}{6}$, and $\frac{11}{12}$?

   f. **6**
   g. **12**
   h. **24**
   j. **36**
   k. **NH**

9. $4^2 - 8 =$

   a. **8**
   b. **0**
   c. **16**
   d. **12**
   e. **NH**

---

5. Which is a pair of prime numbers?

   a. **(2, 29)**
   b. **(4, 7)**
   c. **(5, 14)**
   d. **(3, 27)**
   e. **NH**

10. What is the simplest name for $(9 \times 10^4) + (7 \times 10^3) + (0 \times 10^2) + (0 \times 10) + (5 \times 1)$?

   f. **9,705**
   g. **97,005**
   h. **970,005**
   j. **9,700,005**
   k. **NH**

Directions

Read each question and choose the correct answer. Mark the space for the answer you have chosen. Mark NH if the answer is not here.

---

1. If $\frac{n}{4} = 6$, then $n =$

   a. **28**
   b. **24**
   c. **20**
   d. **16**
   e. **NH**

6. 15 is what percent of 30?

   f. **20%**
   g. **30%**
   h. **40%**
   j. **50%**
   k. **NH**

---

2. If $n = 3$, then $4n - 3 =$

   f. **8**
   g. **9**
   h. **10**
   j. **11**
   k. **NH**

7. If $n - 7 = 9$, then $n =$

   a. **16**
   b. **12**
   c. **8**
   d. **2**
   e. **NH**

---

3. If $n = 4$, then $9n + 7 =$

   a. **43**
   b. **44**
   c. **45**
   d. **46**
   e. **NH**

8. $3,649 \div 80$ is between which numbers?

   f. **10 and 20**
   g. **20 and 30**
   h. **30 and 40**
   j. **40 and 50**
   k. **NH**

---

4. If $\frac{1}{2} = \frac{7}{y}$, then $y =$

   f. **10**
   g. **12**
   h. **14**
   j. **16**
   k. **NH**

9. Which is the subset of the solution set for the inequality $2x > 10$?

   a. **{5, 8, 10}**
   b. **{2, 4, 6}**
   c. **{6, 7, 8}**
   d. **{5, 7, 9}**
   e. **NH**

---

5. Which is the subset of the solution set for the inequality $3x < 24$?

   a. **{0, 2, 4}**
   b. **{4, 5, 8}**
   c. **{4, 6, 8}**
   d. **{6, 7, 8}**
   e. **NH**

10. If $\frac{6}{8} = \frac{h}{24}$, then $h =$

   f. **14**
   g. **16**
   h. **18**
   j. **20**
   k. **NH**

Name _____

Directions

Use the graph to answer the questions. Read each question and choose the correct answer. Mark the space for the answer you have chosen. Mark NH if the answer is not here.

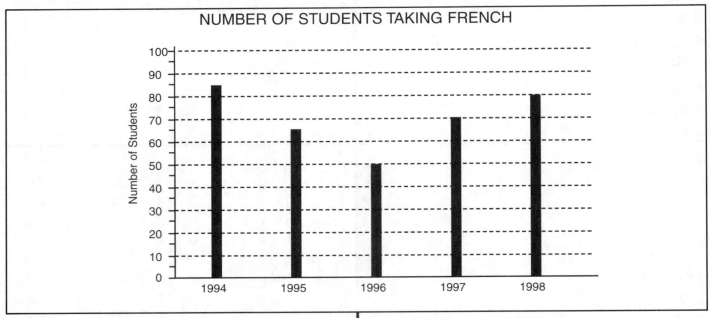

NUMBER OF STUDENTS TAKING FRENCH

1. In which year did the most students take French?

   a. 1994
   b. 1995
   c. 1996
   d. 1998
   e. NH

2. About how many students took French in the years 1997 and 1995 together?

   f. 115
   g. 120
   h. 135
   j. 145
   k. NH

3. In all, about how many students took French in the five years shown on the graph?

   a. 325
   b. 350
   c. 375
   d. 400
   e. NH

4. How many more students took French in 1998 than in 1996?

   f. 15
   g. 20
   h. 25
   j. 30
   k. NH

5. Which two years had the fewest students taking French?

   a. 1994 and 1995
   b. 1995 and 1997
   c. 1996 and 1997
   d. 1997 and 1998
   e. NH

6. What was the average number of students taking French during the five years shown?

   f. 70
   g. 75
   h. 80
   j. 85
   k. NH

Answer Key

Q	Page 1	Page 2	Page 3	Page 4	Page 5	Page 6
1	b	c	b	d	c	b
2	j	j	j	h	g	j
3	d	b	d	c	b	b
4	j	h	f	f	j	h
5	c	a	a	a	c	b
6	f	j	h	g	h	h
7	b	b	a	d	b	d
8	g	j	j	j	f	f
9	d	b	c	c	a	c
10	h	f	j	h	j	h

Q	Page 7	Page 8	Page 9	Page 10	Page 11	Page 12
1	b	c	b	b	c	c
2	f	h	g	f	g	j
3	a	b	c	d	a	a
4	j	h	h	h	f	f
5	a	c	b	c	d	c
6	f	g	g	j	h	h
7	b	d	d	a	b	b
8	g	j	g	g	g	j
9	a	b	b	b	c	d
10	g	g	h	h	j	f

Q	Page 13	Page 14	Page 15	Page 16	Page 17	Page 18
1	c	d	b	b	c	d
2	g	f	g	f	g	f
3	b	b	a	c	a	b
4	f	f	j	f	j	h
5	c	c	d	b	a	a
6	j	j	f	j	j	j
7	d	b	c	c	a	b
8	f	g	g	j	g	g
9	b	b	c	b	a	a
10	h	h	j	f	h	j

Answer Key

Page 19
1. d
2. f
3. b
4. g
5. b
6. j
7. a
8. h
9. a
10. f

Page 20
1. a
2. g
3. b
4. f
5. d
6. j
7. a
8. j
9. d
10. g

Page 21
1. a
2. f
3. c
4. j
5. c
6. j
7. b
8. j
9. b
10. g

Page 22
1. a
2. j
3. a
4. f
5. b
6. h
7. b
8. f
9. d
10. j

Page 23
1. c
2. g
3. b
4. j
5. d
6. f
7. b
8. j
9. b
10. h

Page 24
1. d
2. g
3. a
4. h
5. d
6. f
7. c
8. h
9. b
10. h

Page 25
1. c
2. f
3. a
4. h
5. b
6. j
7. b
8. h
9. a
10. h

Page 26
1. d
2. h
3. a
4. g
5. a
6. f
7. d
8. f
9. c
10. k

Page 27
1. e
2. g
3. e
4. j
5. c
6. j
7. c
8. f
9. b
10. g

Page 28
1. b
2. g
3. c
4. f
5. d
6. h
7. b
8. g
9. c
10. f

Page 29
1. a
2. f
3. a
4. j
5. d
6. h
7. b
8. f
9. d
10. h

Page 30
1. c
2. f
3. a
4. g
5. b
6. j
7. e
8. g
9. a
10. j

Page 31
1. c
2. f
3. b
4. g
5. d
6. j
7. a
8. h
9. c
10. k

Page 32
1. d
2. h
3. b
4. g
5. c
6. h
7. d
8. g
9. c
10. j

Page 33
1. d
2. j
3. a
4. j
5. c
6. j
7. c
8. j
9. d
10. j

Page 34
1. b
2. j
3. d
4. f
5. d
6. j
7. c
8. j
9. a
10. h

Page 35
1. d
2. g
3. c
4. j
5. a
6. j
7. a
8. g
9. b
10. j

Page 36
1. b
2. f
3. c
4. j
5. c
6. h
7. c
8. h
9. a
10. j

Answer Key

Page 37
1. b
2. f
3. d
4. g
5. c
6. f
7. b
8. g
9. d
10. f

Page 38
1. c
2. j
3. b
4. g
5. d
6. j
7. d
8. g
9. c
10. h

Page 39
1. d
2. g
3. e
4. g
5. b
6. h
7. c
8. f
9. b
10. j

Page 40
1. d
2. j
3. b
4. f
5. c
6. g
7. a
8. f
9. c
10. g

Page 41
1. c
2. g
3. a
4. f
5. b
6. f
7. b
8. g
9. d
10. g

Page 42
1. c
2. f
3. c
4. g
5. d
6. h
7. d
8. j
9. c
10. g

Page 43
1. d
2. h
3. c
4. g
5. d
6. f
7. b
8. j
9. b
10. f

Page 44
1. d
2. g
3. b
4. j
5. a
6. h
7. d
8. g
9. c
10. j

Page 45
1. c
2. j
3. b
4. h
5. a
6. h
7. d
8. j
9. b
10. f

Page 46
1. c
2. j
3. e
4. h
5. b
6. j
7. d
8. h
9. a
10. g

Page 47
1. d
2. j
3. d
4. h
5. b
6. g
7. c
8. h
9. b
10. k

Page 48
1. c
2. h
3. d
4. f
5. c
6. h
7. c
8. f
9. c
10. h

Page 49
1. c
2. f
3. b
4. g
5. b
6. j
7. a
8. g
9. a
10. h

Page 50
1. a
2. h
3. d
4. j
5. b
6. g
7. a
8. f
9. d
10. g

Page 51
1. c
2. g
3. a
4. h
5. b
6. j
7. d
8. g
9. b
10. j

Page 52
1. b
2. h
3. d
4. f
5. b
6. j
7. a
8. g
9. b
10. h

Page 53
1. b
2. j
3. c
4. f
5. b
6. f
7. b
8. j
9. a
10. g

Page 54
1. b
2. f
3. a
4. h
5. b
6. j
7. a
8. j
9. d
10. h

Answer Key

Page 55
1. a
2. g
3. d
4. h
5. c
6. g
7. a
8. j
9. c
10. g

Page 56
1. d
2. h
3. d
4. h
5. b
6. g
7. c
8. f
9. c
10. g

Page 57
1. d
2. k
3. b
4. k
5. d
6. h
7. c
8. g
9. b
10. f

Page 58
1. b
2. h
3. c
4. f
5. a
6. f
7. a
8. j
9. b
10. h

Page 59
1. d
2. h
3. c
4. h
5. a
6. g
7. a
8. h
9. c
10. g

Page 60
1. c
2. j
3. a
4. g
5. c
6. g
7. d
8. j
9. c
10. f

Page 61
1. c
2. g
3. d
4. f
5. b
6. h

Page 62
1. e
2. h
3. b
4. g
5. d
6. j

Page 63
1. a
2. j
3. c
4. j
5. d
6. j
7. d
8. f

Page 64
1. d
2. h
3. c
4. f
5. c
6. g
7. d
8. k

Page 65
1. a
2. h
3. b
4. g
5. a
6. g
7. c
8. g

Page 66
1. c
2. h
3. b
4. g
5. b
6. j
7. b
8. h

Page 67
1. c
2. h
3. a
4. g
5. b
6. h
7. d
8. h

Page 68
1. b
2. f
3. c
4. g
5. b
6. h
7. d
8. g

Page 69
1. b
2. h
3. a
4. j
5. a
6. h
7. c
8. f

Page 70
1. d
2. h
3. b
4. h
5. d
6. f
7. b
8. f

Page 71
1. b
2. f
3. c
4. f
5. b
6. h
7. b
8. h

Page 72
1. a
2. h
3. b
4. g
5. a
6. g
7. a
8. h

Answer Key

Page 73
1. a
2. f
3. c
4. g
5. b
6. j
7. a
8. j

Page 74
1. c
2. g
3. f
4. h
5. a
6. j
7. b
8. f

Page 75
1. c
2. f
3. c
4. h
5. a
6. j
7. b
8. j

Page 76
1. d
2. f
3. c
4. g
5. c
6. h
7. b
8. h

Page 77
1. a
2. j
3. c
4. f
5. b
6. j
7. c
8. h

Page 78
1. d
2. h
3. f
4. g
5. b
6. f
7. e
8. h

Page 79
1. d
2. g
3. c
4. f
5. a
6. h
7. b
8. g

Page 80
1. d
2. g
3. c
4. f
5. a
6. g
7. a
8. h

Page 81
1. d
2. g
3. b
4. f
5. d
6. g
7. c
8. j

Page 82
1. d
2. h
3. f
4. h
5. d
6. j
7. b
8. f

Page 83
1. b
2. h
3. f
4. f
5. c
6. h
7. d
8. f

Page 84
1. d
2. j
3. b
4. g
5. d
6. j
7. b
8. g

Page 85
1. c
2. g
3. f
4. g
5. a
6. g
7. d
8. h

Page 86
1. b
2. k
3. d
4. g
5. b
6. f
7. b
8. h

Page 87
1. b
2. h
3. b
4. j
5. a
6. j
7. c
8. g

Page 88
1. a
2. g
3. f
4. h
5. c
6. h
7. b
8. j

Page 89
1. d
2. h
3. c
4. f
5. b
6. j

Page 90
1. d
2. g
3. d
4. k
5. b
6. g

Page 91
1. c
2. j
3. b
4. f
5. b
6. h

Page 92
1. d
2. g
3. c
4. f
5. e
6. j
7. b

Page 93
1. d
2. f
3. d
4. f
5. c
6. k
7. d

Page 94
1. c
2. f
3. c
4. f
5. d
6. h
7. b

Page 95
1. c
2. f
3. c
4. f
5. b
6. j

Page 96
1. b
2. h
3. f
4. g
5. d
6. f

Answer Key

Page 97
1. c
2. g
3. c
4. f
5. b
6. k

Page 98
1. b
2. f
3. a
4. h
5. d
6. g

Page 99
1. a
2. j
3. d
4. g
5. c
6. j
7. a
8. h

Page 100
1. d
2. f
3. b
4. h
5. b
6. j
7. a
8. g

Page 101
1. c
2. g
3. d
4. h
5. c
6. j
7. a
8. f

Page 102
1. d
2. g
3. e
4. h
5. b
6. f
7. c
8. f

Page 103
1. a
2. h
3. b
4. g
5. c
6. h
7. b
8. g

Page 104
1. c
2. h
3. d
4. j
5. d
6. k
7. b
8. f

Page 105
1. b
2. k
3. b
4. g
5. b
6. h
7. a

Page 106
1. e
2. f
3. c
4. j
5. a
6. j

Page 107
1. d
2. h
3. b
4. g
5. c
6. j
7. b
8. f
9. b
10. f

Page 108
1. d
2. k
3. c
4. j
5. a
6. g
7. c
8. f
9. b
10. f

Page 109
1. c
2. j
3. a
4. h
5. b
6. k
7. e
8. g

Page 110
1. b
2. j
3. b
4. g
5. e
6. k
7. b
8. f
9. b
10. g

Page 111
1. b
2. f
3. c
4. f
5. c
6. g
7. c
8. f
9. b
10. h

Page 112
1. a
2. h
3. c
4. g
5. b
6. g
7. c
8. f

Page 113
1. a
2. f
3. b
4. h
5. a
6. g
7. d
8. f
9. a
10. g

Page 114
1. b
2. g
3. a
4. h
5. a
6. j
7. a
8. j
9. c
10. h

Page 115
1. a
2. h
3. b
4. j
5. e
6. f

Answer Sheet

Name _____

Page _____ Score _____

1. ⓐ ⓑ ⓒ ⓓ ⓔ
2. ⓕ ⓖ ⓗ ⓙ ⓚ
3. ⓐ ⓑ ⓒ ⓓ ⓔ
4. ⓕ ⓖ ⓗ ⓙ ⓚ
5. ⓐ ⓑ ⓒ ⓓ ⓔ
6. ⓕ ⓖ ⓗ ⓙ ⓚ
7. ⓐ ⓑ ⓒ ⓓ ⓔ
8. ⓕ ⓖ ⓗ ⓙ ⓚ
9. ⓐ ⓑ ⓒ ⓓ ⓔ
10. ⓕ ⓖ ⓗ ⓙ ⓚ

Page _____ Score _____

1. ⓐ ⓑ ⓒ ⓓ ⓔ
2. ⓕ ⓖ ⓗ ⓙ ⓚ
3. ⓐ ⓑ ⓒ ⓓ ⓔ
4. ⓕ ⓖ ⓗ ⓙ ⓚ
5. ⓐ ⓑ ⓒ ⓓ ⓔ
6. ⓕ ⓖ ⓗ ⓙ ⓚ
7. ⓐ ⓑ ⓒ ⓓ ⓔ
8. ⓕ ⓖ ⓗ ⓙ ⓚ
9. ⓐ ⓑ ⓒ ⓓ ⓔ
10. ⓕ ⓖ ⓗ ⓙ ⓚ

Page _____ Score _____

1. ⓐ ⓑ ⓒ ⓓ ⓔ
2. ⓕ ⓖ ⓗ ⓙ ⓚ
3. ⓐ ⓑ ⓒ ⓓ ⓔ
4. ⓕ ⓖ ⓗ ⓙ ⓚ
5. ⓐ ⓑ ⓒ ⓓ ⓔ
6. ⓕ ⓖ ⓗ ⓙ ⓚ
7. ⓐ ⓑ ⓒ ⓓ ⓔ
8. ⓕ ⓖ ⓗ ⓙ ⓚ
9. ⓐ ⓑ ⓒ ⓓ ⓔ
10. ⓕ ⓖ ⓗ ⓙ ⓚ

Page _____ Score _____

1. ⓐ ⓑ ⓒ ⓓ ⓔ
2. ⓕ ⓖ ⓗ ⓙ ⓚ
3. ⓐ ⓑ ⓒ ⓓ ⓔ
4. ⓕ ⓖ ⓗ ⓙ ⓚ
5. ⓐ ⓑ ⓒ ⓓ ⓔ
6. ⓕ ⓖ ⓗ ⓙ ⓚ
7. ⓐ ⓑ ⓒ ⓓ ⓔ
8. ⓕ ⓖ ⓗ ⓙ ⓚ
9. ⓐ ⓑ ⓒ ⓓ ⓔ
10. ⓕ ⓖ ⓗ ⓙ ⓚ

Page _____ Score _____

1. ⓐ ⓑ ⓒ ⓓ ⓔ
2. ⓕ ⓖ ⓗ ⓙ ⓚ
3. ⓐ ⓑ ⓒ ⓓ ⓔ
4. ⓕ ⓖ ⓗ ⓙ ⓚ
5. ⓐ ⓑ ⓒ ⓓ ⓔ
6. ⓕ ⓖ ⓗ ⓙ ⓚ
7. ⓐ ⓑ ⓒ ⓓ ⓔ
8. ⓕ ⓖ ⓗ ⓙ ⓚ
9. ⓐ ⓑ ⓒ ⓓ ⓔ
10. ⓕ ⓖ ⓗ ⓙ ⓚ

Page _____ Score _____

1. ⓐ ⓑ ⓒ ⓓ ⓔ
2. ⓕ ⓖ ⓗ ⓙ ⓚ
3. ⓐ ⓑ ⓒ ⓓ ⓔ
4. ⓕ ⓖ ⓗ ⓙ ⓚ
5. ⓐ ⓑ ⓒ ⓓ ⓔ
6. ⓕ ⓖ ⓗ ⓙ ⓚ
7. ⓐ ⓑ ⓒ ⓓ ⓔ
8. ⓕ ⓖ ⓗ ⓙ ⓚ
9. ⓐ ⓑ ⓒ ⓓ ⓔ
10. ⓕ ⓖ ⓗ ⓙ ⓚ

Page _____ Score _____

1. ⓐ ⓑ ⓒ ⓓ ⓔ
2. ⓕ ⓖ ⓗ ⓙ ⓚ
3. ⓐ ⓑ ⓒ ⓓ ⓔ
4. ⓕ ⓖ ⓗ ⓙ ⓚ
5. ⓐ ⓑ ⓒ ⓓ ⓔ
6. ⓕ ⓖ ⓗ ⓙ ⓚ
7. ⓐ ⓑ ⓒ ⓓ ⓔ
8. ⓕ ⓖ ⓗ ⓙ ⓚ
9. ⓐ ⓑ ⓒ ⓓ ⓔ
10. ⓕ ⓖ ⓗ ⓙ ⓚ

Page _____ Score _____

1. ⓐ ⓑ ⓒ ⓓ ⓔ
2. ⓕ ⓖ ⓗ ⓙ ⓚ
3. ⓐ ⓑ ⓒ ⓓ ⓔ
4. ⓕ ⓖ ⓗ ⓙ ⓚ
5. ⓐ ⓑ ⓒ ⓓ ⓔ
6. ⓕ ⓖ ⓗ ⓙ ⓚ
7. ⓐ ⓑ ⓒ ⓓ ⓔ
8. ⓕ ⓖ ⓗ ⓙ ⓚ
9. ⓐ ⓑ ⓒ ⓓ ⓔ
10. ⓕ ⓖ ⓗ ⓙ ⓚ

Page _____ Score _____

1. ⓐ ⓑ ⓒ ⓓ ⓔ
2. ⓕ ⓖ ⓗ ⓙ ⓚ
3. ⓐ ⓑ ⓒ ⓓ ⓔ
4. ⓕ ⓖ ⓗ ⓙ ⓚ
5. ⓐ ⓑ ⓒ ⓓ ⓔ
6. ⓕ ⓖ ⓗ ⓙ ⓚ
7. ⓐ ⓑ ⓒ ⓓ ⓔ
8. ⓕ ⓖ ⓗ ⓙ ⓚ
9. ⓐ ⓑ ⓒ ⓓ ⓔ
10. ⓕ ⓖ ⓗ ⓙ ⓚ

Answer Sheet

Name _____

Page _____ Score _____	Page _____ Score _____	Page _____ Score _____
1. ⓐ ⓑ ⓒ ⓓ ⓔ	1. ⓐ ⓑ ⓒ ⓓ ⓔ	1. ⓐ ⓑ ⓒ ⓓ ⓔ
2. ⓕ ⓖ ⓗ ⓙ ⓚ	2. ⓕ ⓖ ⓗ ⓙ ⓚ	2. ⓕ ⓖ ⓗ ⓙ ⓚ
3. ⓐ ⓑ ⓒ ⓓ ⓔ	3. ⓐ ⓑ ⓒ ⓓ ⓔ	3. ⓐ ⓑ ⓒ ⓓ ⓔ
4. ⓕ ⓖ ⓗ ⓙ ⓚ	4. ⓕ ⓖ ⓗ ⓙ ⓚ	4. ⓕ ⓖ ⓗ ⓙ ⓚ
5. ⓐ ⓑ ⓒ ⓓ ⓔ	5. ⓐ ⓑ ⓒ ⓓ ⓔ	5. ⓐ ⓑ ⓒ ⓓ ⓔ
6. ⓕ ⓖ ⓗ ⓙ ⓚ	6. ⓕ ⓖ ⓗ ⓙ ⓚ	6. ⓕ ⓖ ⓗ ⓙ ⓚ
7. ⓐ ⓑ ⓒ ⓓ ⓔ	7. ⓐ ⓑ ⓒ ⓓ ⓔ	7. ⓐ ⓑ ⓒ ⓓ ⓔ
8. ⓕ ⓖ ⓗ ⓙ ⓚ	8. ⓕ ⓖ ⓗ ⓙ ⓚ	8. ⓕ ⓖ ⓗ ⓙ ⓚ
9. ⓐ ⓑ ⓒ ⓓ ⓔ	9. ⓐ ⓑ ⓒ ⓓ ⓔ	9. ⓐ ⓑ ⓒ ⓓ ⓔ
10. ⓕ ⓖ ⓗ ⓙ ⓚ	10. ⓕ ⓖ ⓗ ⓙ ⓚ	10. ⓕ ⓖ ⓗ ⓙ ⓚ
Page _____ Score _____	Page _____ Score _____	Page _____ Score _____
1. ⓐ ⓑ ⓒ ⓓ ⓔ	1. ⓐ ⓑ ⓒ ⓓ ⓔ	1. ⓐ ⓑ ⓒ ⓓ ⓔ
2. ⓕ ⓖ ⓗ ⓙ ⓚ	2. ⓕ ⓖ ⓗ ⓙ ⓚ	2. ⓕ ⓖ ⓗ ⓙ ⓚ
3. ⓐ ⓑ ⓒ ⓓ ⓔ	3. ⓐ ⓑ ⓒ ⓓ ⓔ	3. ⓐ ⓑ ⓒ ⓓ ⓔ
4. ⓕ ⓖ ⓗ ⓙ ⓚ	4. ⓕ ⓖ ⓗ ⓙ ⓚ	4. ⓕ ⓖ ⓗ ⓙ ⓚ
5. ⓐ ⓑ ⓒ ⓓ ⓔ	5. ⓐ ⓑ ⓒ ⓓ ⓔ	5. ⓐ ⓑ ⓒ ⓓ ⓔ
6. ⓕ ⓖ ⓗ ⓙ ⓚ	6. ⓕ ⓖ ⓗ ⓙ ⓚ	6. ⓕ ⓖ ⓗ ⓙ ⓚ
7. ⓐ ⓑ ⓒ ⓓ ⓔ	7. ⓐ ⓑ ⓒ ⓓ ⓔ	7. ⓐ ⓑ ⓒ ⓓ ⓔ
8. ⓕ ⓖ ⓗ ⓙ ⓚ	8. ⓕ ⓖ ⓗ ⓙ ⓚ	8. ⓕ ⓖ ⓗ ⓙ ⓚ
9. ⓐ ⓑ ⓒ ⓓ ⓔ	9. ⓐ ⓑ ⓒ ⓓ ⓔ	9. ⓐ ⓑ ⓒ ⓓ ⓔ
10. ⓕ ⓖ ⓗ ⓙ ⓚ	10. ⓕ ⓖ ⓗ ⓙ ⓚ	10. ⓕ ⓖ ⓗ ⓙ ⓚ
Page _____ Score _____	Page _____ Score _____	Page _____ Score _____
1. ⓐ ⓑ ⓒ ⓓ ⓔ	1. ⓐ ⓑ ⓒ ⓓ ⓔ	1. ⓐ ⓑ ⓒ ⓓ ⓔ
2. ⓕ ⓖ ⓗ ⓙ ⓚ	2. ⓕ ⓖ ⓗ ⓙ ⓚ	2. ⓕ ⓖ ⓗ ⓙ ⓚ
3. ⓐ ⓑ ⓒ ⓓ ⓔ	3. ⓐ ⓑ ⓒ ⓓ ⓔ	3. ⓐ ⓑ ⓒ ⓓ ⓔ
4. ⓕ ⓖ ⓗ ⓙ ⓚ	4. ⓕ ⓖ ⓗ ⓙ ⓚ	4. ⓕ ⓖ ⓗ ⓙ ⓚ
5. ⓐ ⓑ ⓒ ⓓ ⓔ	5. ⓐ ⓑ ⓒ ⓓ ⓔ	5. ⓐ ⓑ ⓒ ⓓ ⓔ
6. ⓕ ⓖ ⓗ ⓙ ⓚ	6. ⓕ ⓖ ⓗ ⓙ ⓚ	6. ⓕ ⓖ ⓗ ⓙ ⓚ
7. ⓐ ⓑ ⓒ ⓓ ⓔ	7. ⓐ ⓑ ⓒ ⓓ ⓔ	7. ⓐ ⓑ ⓒ ⓓ ⓔ
8. ⓕ ⓖ ⓗ ⓙ ⓚ	8. ⓕ ⓖ ⓗ ⓙ ⓚ	8. ⓕ ⓖ ⓗ ⓙ ⓚ
9. ⓐ ⓑ ⓒ ⓓ ⓔ	9. ⓐ ⓑ ⓒ ⓓ ⓔ	9. ⓐ ⓑ ⓒ ⓓ ⓔ
10. ⓕ ⓖ ⓗ ⓙ ⓚ	10. ⓕ ⓖ ⓗ ⓙ ⓚ	10. ⓕ ⓖ ⓗ ⓙ ⓚ